Taking Charge of Your Destiny to Succeed

Challenges and Triumphs

This book chronicles the extraordinary journey of a man who overcomes immense challenges to achieve extraordinary personal and professional success.

Dr. Mehdi Khosrow-Pour

Published by

eContent Pro International Press

New York | London | Beijing

Published in the United States of America by
eContent Pro International Press
250 Broadway, Suite 620
New York, NY 10007, USA
Tel: 717-533-4010
Fax: 717-533-7115
Web site: www.ecppress.com

CREDITS
Publisher: eContent Pro International Press
Editor: Jennifer Neidig & Dr. Amy Samuelson
Cover Design: Phillip Shickler
Typesetting: Phillip Shickler
Cover Photography: Kristina Byrne

Copyright © 2026 by eContent Pro International Press. All rights reserved. No part of this work may be reproduced or used in any form or by any means- graphic, electronic, or mechanical, including photocopying, recording, taping, or information and retrieval system-without written permission from the publisher.

Library of Congress Catalogue In-Publication Data
eContent Pro International Press

Taking Charge of Your Destiny to Succeed: Challenges and Triumphs.
The journey of a man who overcomes immense challenges to
achieve extraordinary personal and professional success.

ISBN: 979-8-8965-0003-2
EISBN: 979-8-8965-0004-9

Classification:

Disclaimer: The content of this book is based on the author's recollections and may contain some inaccuracies regarding names, dates, places, etc. The author has made every effort to provide the most accurate information based on his memories. Any inaccuracies are purely unintentional.

Dedication

This book is dedicated to the memory of my late mother and father for the love and devotion they displayed for their children. Not only did they teach me the importance of hard work and determination, but they also instilled in me the value of humanitarianism.

My book is also dedicated to my wife, Olga, and our sons, Darius and Cyrus. They have filled my life with great love, joy, and happiness. In our household, the saying is: "Our boys are handsome and smart, Mommy is beautiful and smart, and Daddy is simply lucky!" I am truly blessed and fortunate to share this gift with them.

Chronicle and Acknowledgement

I would not have written this book without the continuous encouragement of my wife, Olga Khosrow-Pour. I feel a sense of responsibility and pride knowing that she believes that sharing my experiences and thoughts can empower our sons, Darius and Cyrus, as well as other readers around the world. I hope to inspire others to believe in themselves and recognize their own potential, helping them discover that hard work, commitment, determination, and a positive attitude can make their dreams a reality!

The planning and writing of this book took nearly eight years. During that time, I was lucky to have the support of many individuals. In 2017, Ms. Lindsay Wertman helped me write the manuscript's first version, recording and transcribing each chapter as I commuted back and forth between New York and Pennsylvania. I wish to acknowledge her efforts and dedication.

There were several pauses throughout the course of this project. However, I returned to it in early 2021, collaborating with professional ghost writers Ms. Rachel Gostenhofer and Mr. Tom Hanlon. Regrettably, my experience with both the professional ghost writers and the Gotham Ghostwriters Agency in New York City was unproductive, so I decided to move forward myself.

By early November 2023, I became heavily involved in writing this book, completing the first draft in its entirety by February 2024. Shortly after its completion, I asked Ms. Jennifer Neidig and later Dr. Amy Samuelson to conduct a comprehensive paid copyediting and proofreading of the manuscript. I would like to express my thanks to both of them for their assistance in enriching this book.

I also appreciate Mr. Nick Newcomer, Ms. Courtney Mengel, and Mr. Phil Shickler for their efforts and support. As stated, Olga, the love of my life, deserves my outmost gratitude for her encouragement and moral support.

Finally, many thanks to all those individuals who have helped me along the way. Your lessons have taught me to become an upstanding and respectable human being who does not take anything for granted!

Table of Contents

Preface 9

Chapter 1: *The Dream Bike* 13

Chapter 2: *A Matter of Survival* 23

Chapter 3: *Pushing the Boulder* 35

Chapter 4: *Swimming Upstream* 47

Chapter 5: *Coming to America* 67

Chapter 6: *My Academic Journey* 91

Chapter 7: *Interruption in My Education Because of a Revolution* 111

Chapter 8: *My Academic Career* 133

Chapter 9: *My Life as an Entrepreneur* 153

Chapter 10: *A Successful Life* 177

Chapter 11: *Freedom is not for Free* 195

Chapter 12: *Charity Work and Responsibility* 213

Chapter 13: *Summary and Lessons Learned* 231

Preface

Throughout history, there have been many stories of individuals from all over the world who have managed to achieve extraordinary triumph in their lives, turning obstacles into paths of opportunity and, ultimately, success. The stories of individuals like Nelson Mandela, a South African revolutionary and politician, and Mother Teresa, a Catholic nun and missionary in India, are the ultimate proof of resiliency and the ability to overcome unimaginable challenges.

In more modern times, the life stories of icons like Steve Jobs, influential businessman and co-founder of Apple, Inc.; Bill Gates, philanthropist and co-founder of Microsoft; Stephen Hawking, English theoretical physicist and mathematician; Michael Phelps, American swimmer and the most decorated Olympian (with 28 medals); Jeff Bezos, founder of Amazon and Blue Origin; and Warren Buffet, American investor and CEO of Berkshire Hathaway, offer clear evidence that the combination of knowledge, hard work, and determination can bring success and extraordinary achievements.

Like many children, I was always driven to explore new opportunities. However, growing up poor and dealing with countless challenges and hurdles—like the loss of my mother and not being able to attend normal educational programs like the other kids my age—made my life difficult and often unbearable. As I reflect on my childhood in Iran, I realize that, even at a young age, there was a part of me that was unwilling to accept the "status quo" or the destiny I was handed. And, although my path was scattered with roadblocks, I was able to find bright paths in some of the darkest moments of my formative years.

One of the first lessons I learned in my journey to self-discovery focused on my pursuit of excellence. By studying hard, I wanted to achieve the highest grades among my more than 5,000 elementary school peers, striving to earn the used bicycle that my father had promised me. That bicycle was going to offer me a glimpse into a world with limitless adventures and untapped freedoms.

While my dream of riding that blue bicycle out of the store was crushed, it taught me my second lesson in self-discovery—that with determination, you can overcome hurdles (even when faced with adversity)!

Throughout my childhood, I also learned the importance of education, a value instilled in me by my father. It became a driving force throughout my life, allowing me to access many opportunities, guiding me toward my goals, and even helping me identify alternative paths to reach my destination.

With focus and self-discipline, I dedicated countless hours to odd jobs and my studies, putting myself through school and, ultimately, earning my baccalaureate degree, two graduate master's degrees, and my doctorate. Further down the line, I became a successful university professor, researcher, and department chair at a respected American university. Eventually, I used my education and tenacity to become a productive and successful entrepreneur and philanthropist.

My father was always my idol, working tirelessly to try and open doors to new possibilities for his children. Although he was illiterate and unable to read or write, my father was determined to make sure his children would not face the same limitations he dealt with in life. He taught me the value of hard work, self-discipline, perseverance, lifelong learning, and the art of business. His sacrifices set the foundation for my future decisions and taught me so much of what is captured in this book.

My mother and grandmother, with their boundless love and support, showed me the meaning of compassion. They reminded me to be humble, kind, and hopeful—no matter how challenging the road ahead. Though they were a part of my life for only a short time, their impact was profound. This book is a tribute to their legacy.

My children are the primary reason I wrote this book. They are my greatest source of joy and inspiration, and I want them to know their father's life story. In these pages, they can learn about where their own father came from. They will understand the struggles and successes that shaped their father's life. And they can carry forward the values, knowledge, and hard work that have guided me.

Writing this book has allowed me to document my story for them—to show them that with hard work and determination, you can achieve your dreams. It chronicles my commitment to my family and my respect for my father, the insights I gained as an immigrant to the United States, my hunger for realizing my dreams, and how I found purpose in my journey.

I also wrote this book to inspire others who might find themselves at the starting line of their journey. Perhaps you, too, are faced with adversities, challenges, and setbacks as you navigate through life and try your hardest to build a successful career or financial freedom. With education, hard work, and determination, you can achieve far beyond what you might imagine. Instead of underestimating your ability and submitting to life's limitations, you can overcome any challenges by using the principles I define in this book and have utilized to realize success. My story is a testament to the power of these principles.

I owe a debt of gratitude to my parents, wife, children, friends, mentors, colleagues, and employees, who have supported me every step of the way. To those who read this book, I hope my story serves as a source of motivation. May you find the courage to ride your metaphorical bike toward your dreams and the resilience to overcome any barriers in your path. Believe in yourself and in all those undiscovered abilities within you to travel through your life's various roads.

Above all, I reiterate the lesson given to me by my mother and grandmother: Be compassionate and have empathy for those who are less fortunate than you on this earth—for they will inspire respect, create a supportive community, and enrich your own journey.

Chapter 1
The Dream Bike

The used bicycle shop was small, crammed between a small deli and a shoe store. It was on the way to my elementary school in Tehran. My whole way to school was lined with tiny shops and street vendors selling fruits, vegetables, toys, and other wares.

The shop itself held only about 10 bikes. All used, all refurbished, all cleaned up, and ready to sell.

Nothing about the shop was special—except for one thing.

That royal blue Schwinn, the one on the end. The one with the stainless handlebars and brake levers on the bars. Every morning on my way to school, I stopped at the shop's window and stared at the bike. I quickly dismissed all the other options; this was the only bike for me. Motorbikes zipped by, their engines annoyingly loud; sometimes the riders blared their horns as they passed other riders. People walked by, talking, shouting, laughing. It was all background noise to me. The smells of the street foods—kabab on sticks, cooked beets, cooked lentils with onions—wafted through the air and found my nose. But it did not deter me.

All I could see was me riding that blue bike, cruising through the city streets, going wherever my heart desired. I blocked out everything else.

That blue bike, I realize now, represented a certain type of freedom for me. It awakened a hope in me, a desire. And there was only one way it would be fulfilled.

"Come on," my neighborhood friend, Reza, said as we walked to school. "We're going to be late."

"Hold on a minute," I'd reply, not taking my eyes off the—off my—bike. Reluctantly, I would tear myself away from the shop and trudge on to school. My favorite part of school had nothing to do with learning or my classmates. It had everything to do with that used Schwinn.

As a 12-year-old, my thoughts were consumed by that bike.

I had to have it.

"I tell you what," my father, Gohlam Hussein, said one evening after I told him how special that bike was and how badly I wanted—needed—it. "If you do well on your examination, I will go down to that shop and buy that bike for you." In Iran in the 1960s, every elementary school student had to take a middle school examination after completing sixth grade to be able to move on in their high school education. The exam was quite grueling, lasting three to four hours.

"Thank you, Dad, but that exam is three months away," I said, disappointed.

"I can't help that. It will give you something to work toward," he replied. "Do you want the bike or not?"

I quickly nodded. "Yes, very much."

"Then you study hard, and I'll get you that bike."

He saw the overjoyed look on my face and gave me a stern look.

"But only," he said, wagging a finger at me, "if you do well on that exam and if the price is what I can afford."

I nodded and ran off. I didn't want to tempt fate. I didn't want him rethinking what he'd just said.

That night, as I lay in the bed that I shared with my younger brother, Mohammad, it took longer than normal to fall asleep. While discouraged that I had to wait a few months to get the bike, it also gave me something to look forward to. It gave me hope, direction, and purpose.

Today, I find it amazing how far those three concepts can take you.

To understand the importance of that bike, you need to understand a few things about my early life.

First, we were poor. My father never attended a day of school in his life; he was completely illiterate and learned to sign his name by drawing the letters. He married my mother, his cousin, when he was 15. She was 13. As with most marriages at that time, especially in rural areas of Iran, the marriage was arranged. My father, along with another fellow, owned a tiny shop in southcentral Tehran. They sold rice and dried vegetables and fruits like chickpeas, lentils, dates, and raisins. The shop barely produced enough income for my father and his partner to support their families.

Second, we lived in the southern section of Tehran, which was a poor area of the city. To be both poor and living in a developing country meant essentially all your income went to your very elemental needs: food and shelter. My father was a hard worker throughout his entire life. He ran his shop with his business partner, but to make ends meet with no education in a developing country—supporting himself, his wife, his five living children (two died, one in childbirth and the other at six months), and his mother in-law was not an easy task. So, you can understand why he didn't just say, "Yes, let's go buy that bike right now." To have even a used bike could be considered an extravagance; he was probably looking at it in terms of money that could be better spent on groceries, rent, or clothes.

Third, Dad emphasized education, for the very reason that he didn't have one. He knew firsthand what a struggle it was to provide for a family–to have a decent life–without one. He knew well the life of an illiterate person whose choices of work and opportunities for any sort of livable income were severely limited. He did not want that life for his children. And he knew that the way out of that cycle of poverty, the only hope, was to go as far as you could with your education, to harness the power of your mind and elevate yourself above the masses of illiterate people who worked in the bazaars of Tehran. In those days, the illiteracy rate in Iran was about 76%—an unbelievable rate. Essentially everyone who grew up outside of large cities was illiterate. So, throughout our childhoods, he harped to all of us kids about working hard in school. He wanted a better life for us.

Fourth, my father ruled with an iron fist. What he said was law. You didn't question him; you didn't argue with him; you didn't talk back to him. This wasn't just his nature; it is and has been one of the core tenets of Iranian culture stretching back for millennia. The male-dominated culture, of course, stems from Islamic beliefs and laws.

So, to me, that bike was a treasure, one that would bring me freedom.

But while I saw that blue bike as a treasure, one that not only symbolized but in some small ways would grant me freedom, my father saw it as a means to incentivize studying hard, getting a good exam score, and moving on toward the larger goal of continuing my education and bettering my life. If I met his goal, he would reward me.

I was determined to meet his goal, and I did—and then some.

I finished with the second-highest score on the exam out of about 5,000 middle schoolers in the district. I could not wait for the day to end when my father would come home, and I could share the good news with him. But Dad always worked late, making my anticipation extremely painful. Finally, when he came home, I ran up to him.

"Dad! Dad! Look at my score!" I said, holding my exam report in front of him before realizing how silly that was: He couldn't read it. "My teacher said it was the second-highest score in the entire district! He said there are about five thousand kids who took the same test, and only one got a higher score!"

My dad smiled, but he looked at my older brother Ali, who was nearby. Ali glanced at my exam report and nodded, affirming what I said. "Good job, little brother," he said. Ali was seven years older than me, and he was still living at home at the time.

This time, my father's smile was a bit more relaxed, a bit broader. I'm sure he trusted me, but it has to be hard to never be able to discern something for yourself because you can't read.

"That's good, Mehdi," he said.

"So, when can we go?" I said, hope and excitement rising in my voice.

"Go? Go where?"

"To the bike shop! Remember?"

He nodded. "Oh, right. We can go tomorrow. You come down to my shop and we can go from there."

I wanted to ask why we couldn't go now, but I didn't want to make him mad. I knew I wouldn't change his mind. I sighed and said okay. That night, I kept seeing visions of that blue bike in my head. I had passed it every day on the way to and from school; it hadn't been sold. I couldn't understand why someone hadn't bought it yet; it was so sleek and snazzy, clearly the best bike in the shop.

And then the thought struck me: What if someone bought it today, after I passed it on the way home? What if we go to the shop tomorrow, and my blue bike is gone?

I pushed that thought out of my mind and struggled to fall asleep, anxious for a new dawn to break.

The next morning, I asked my father if I could come to his shop with him and we could go from there to the bike shop. He told me to wait for a few hours so he could get things in order in his shop and make sure that his business partner was there. His partner often showed up late.

So, I waited a few hours, though each minute seemed like an hour. Finally, I ran to my dad's shop—not far from the bike shop. He told his partner that he was leaving for a bit, and we walked to the bike shop. I had looked at that bike countless times, but had never been inside the shop. Now, stepping inside, it was almost like entering a sacred place.

For those of you who have not been to Iran, understand that there is a haggling system—*chaaneh zadan* in Farsi (the official language spoken in the country)—that has been in place virtually forever. Chaaneh, or "chin," reflects the constant movement of the chin and mouth when buyers and sellers haggle on a price of an item. With some exceptions, such as retail groceries or restaurant and hotel bills, almost everything in Iran is negotiable. If you don't know how to haggle—how to jockey back and forth on the price of an item—chances are you will pay well over what you could have paid for the item.

Of course, my father, having worked since he was 14, was quite experienced in chaaneh zadan. He walked up to the shop owner, an older man with wrinkled skin, white hair, and pouchy bags under his dark eyes.

"*Salam*," my father said. Salam, which translates to "peace," is commonly used as a greeting (much like "hello" is used in the United States.).

The old man smiled, returned the peaceful greeting, and shook hands with my father. "Be my guest," he said.

"We are interested in a bike." Dad turned and looked at me. "Which one, Mehdi?"

"The blue one," I said, pointing to the bike at the end of the row.

"Ah, this one!" the shopkeeper said, coming to life now. He patted the seat of the bike. "Yes, this one is a very good bike. Your son has a good eye."

"How much is the bike?" my father asked.

"No, no. First, let him take it for a test ride," the shopkeeper said. "You go, ride the bike up and down the street. Make sure you like it." He smiled at me confidently, apparently certain that I would like it.

"But first, the price," my father said.

"Let the boy ride," the shopkeeper said. "Whether you buy the bike or not, let him enjoy it a minute. Then, we can talk price."

I needed no more encouragement. I wheeled the bike outside, weaving between people on the sidewalk. Once in the street, I mounted it and took off. My father and the shopkeeper came out to watch me go up and down the street a few times. Though I had never owned a bike before, my good friend, Davood, had taught me how to ride on his dad's old bike.

The bike was everything I had dreamed of. It rode so smoothly! I could imagine myself flying down streets and roads, the wind whipping through my hair, the sun shining on my face, the road a blur beneath my tires. This bike would be my ticket to a freedom that I had yet to experience. By the time I stopped and returned the bike to the shop owner, my heart was pounding—not from the exertion, but from the excitement of getting the bike.

Back in the store, my father got right to the point. "Okay, how much?"

"It's a good bike. Tires good, chain replaced. Very sturdy bike," the shop owner said. He looked at me. "You like it? Good ride?"

"Yes. Very good ride."

"How much?" my father repeated.

"Oh, a bike like this, many people have come in to buy it. But they don't want to pay fair price," the shop owner lamented.

"How much?" my father persisted.

The old man stroked his chin as if in deep thought. Then he named a price equivalent to US$120 in Iranian currency (rials).

My father shook his head, looking disappointed. "No, no, this bike is used. Look, the paint is chipped here."

"That little chip doesn't affect the bike, sir, no way," the shopkeeper said. "It's a fair price."

"I will pay 80 dollars, no more," my father said.

The shopkeeper's eyebrows shot up in surprise. "Eighty dollars? For a bike like this? I'm giving you a deal at 120, believe me. Much more expensive at other shops."

They went back and forth like this for a while. Like watching a tennis match, my head swiveled from Dad to the shopkeeper and then back to my dad. The shopkeeper grudgingly lowered his price a bit, and my dad just as grudgingly upped his offer a bit. They kept moving closer to an agreed-upon price. Finally, the shopkeeper said, "Okay, 100 dollars. My final offer."

My dad shook his head. "I will give you 95 for it."

The shopkeeper smiled sadly. "I'm sorry, but I cannot sell it for that price."

Fearing that the bike that I had so long desired—and had now ridden—was slipping away, I brashly interjected. "Dad! It's only five dollars! One hundred is a good price for it."

It felt like the world had stopped spinning for a moment. Or, rather, like it had come to a crashing halt. The shopkeeper said nothing, taking a respectful step back. He could see what was happening between father and son.

And what was happening between father and son was that I was going to get the talking-to of my life. My father immediately stopped his negotiation with the shopkeeper and told him firmly that we had to leave. He grabbed me by the wrist before walking me out of the bicycle store. He placed his hand firmly on my shoulder as he guided me back down to his tiny shop, several blocks away. He didn't say a word as we walked, but even the people we passed on the street could see what was going on and gave us a wide berth as we made our way back to his shop.

Once inside the shop, my father took me toward the back and then spun me around so we were facing each other. He was red-faced and livid, and he slapped me—hard—on the cheek. It's the only time he ever laid a hand on me.

"Don't you ever do that again!" he shouted. "You do not speak when two adults are bargaining! Do you hear me?"

I would've had to have been deaf not to hear him. It was more likely that I would go deaf because he was shouting so loud.

"Yes, Dad," I said, fighting back tears. I wanted to touch where he had slapped me; my face was stinging. But I didn't want to give him the satisfaction of showing him that it hurt.

He yelled a little bit more, then told me to go home. I was happy to get out of there. Away from him, my tears flowed freely as I anguished over how close I had been to getting that bike, and how I had blown it.

Just like that, the freedom that it had promised had vanished.

Chapter 2
A Matter of Survival

My parents were born and raised in Langarood, a coastal village in Gilan Province on the south coast of the Caspian Sea (which is, in fact, the world's largest lake rather than a sea). Langarood, which translates to "the lower limb of the river," boasts the Langarood River, cutting between the lush rolling hills and white sandy beaches of the village. It's an idyllic place to live. Today, it is a flourishing tourist attraction, with a population of about 80,000 people.

Despite the beauty of the village, there was nothing idyllic about my parents' lives. Dad lost his parents at an early age and was adopted by his uncle. This uncle was also my mother's father, meaning my dad and his future wife were cousins.

Every day, my father would get up early, eat bread and feta cheese, drink some tea, and go to work crafting wooden sandals and shoes that his uncle would then sell in the local markets. Slicing rubber from old car tires and forging them into shoe straps was tedious work. His hands became dry, then calloused as he worked with a hammer, awl, knife, cutter, and thread up to 14 hours a day. They did not look like the hands of a 15-year-old boy.

Dad took it all in stride. He did the work that was in front of him, careful not to look too far ahead or ponder the past. He kept the steady pace of a cobbler. At the end of the day, he would drop onto his thin mattress on the floor of his uncle's home.

Marrying at a young age—just 13 and 15 years of age for my parents—was common, especially in rural areas and villages of Iran. Interfamily marriages, or marriages between cousins and other relatives, were also very common and rooted in culture and society. In some families, it was a way to strengthen familial bonds, creating a more cohesive unit. These arrangements also provided economic stability.

My parents' first child died at birth, when my mother was 15 years old. The next year, my parents welcomed my eldest brother, Ali, followed by my sister, Zahra (Zari). I was born in June 1951, following the death of their second daughter. I also had two younger brothers, Mohammad and Ahmad.

My second sister died at six months old from carbon monoxide poisoning. To stay warm in the winter, Ali, Zari, and the baby slept on an eight-by-eight-foot low, large wooden table. The room was heated by charcoal in a pit underneath the table, and a large blanket was placed on the top to keep out the cold. According to my maternal grandmother, who was living with us at the time, the baby got too far underneath the blanket. With just a small opening, carbon monoxide crept beneath the covering, suffocating my sister.

When I was six months old, Dad moved the family from Langarood to Tehran, convinced he could make a better living than his handcrafted footwear provided. The big city also offered better access to education.

We lived on the second floor of a two-story house. My father's friend occupied the first floor. We had two bedrooms and our own kitchenette. The neighborhood was congested and poor, with rows of adjoining houses and storefronts. Some people made their meager living pulling rickshaw-like carts through the streets, transporting goods to the shops.

My brother Ali (12 years old), me (5 years old), and Grandmother*

*Under Islmaic Laws a face or any uncovered body parts of a female should not be depicted to strangers.

We lived with my maternal grandmother. She was warm and kind; I loved her greatly. My grandmother lost her husband after the two of them had five children (one boy and four girls). However, my mother was her only living child at that time. The daughter of my mother's dead sister, our aunt, also lived with us.

After 10 years, we moved again, settling in southcentral Tehran, where my father had scraped together enough savings to build a moderate home for his family. When I wasn't in school, I played soccer on a dirt field with the neighborhood kids. I remember walking home along the gravel roads, my face and clothes covered in dust from our games.

My father continued to put in long hours to ensure that we had food on our table. We ate rice with every meal, much like potatoes are a staple in the Western world. We never refused to eat what my mother prepared. We were just thankful for our meal—it was literally a matter of survival.

While he was not a religious man, Dad followed Zakat, a form of almsgiving and one of the five pillars of the Muslim faith. Knowing what it was like to be poor, he never hesitated to help those in need. On several occasions, I saw him visiting our neighbors with spare goods like rice, cooking oil, and beans. He would knock on the door, present the food, wish the person as-salamu alaikum (peace be upon you), and walk away.

One day, Dad looked at me and said, "Never sell your soul to money, Mehdi." Here was a man who had struggled his entire life. Yet he was also a man dedicated to meeting the needs of others. Dad valued making human connections and aimed to find purpose beyond making money. I admired his compassion.

My grandmother, on the other hand, was very religious, awakening before sunrise to perform her daily morning prayers. The second pillar of Islam, *Salah* (or prayer), requires that Muslims wash their hands, face, and feet before praying. Inside the mosque, a caller chants as verses from the Quran, the holy book for Muslims, are recited aloud or in silence. Prayers take place facing Mecca, the capital of Mecca Province in Saudi Arabia and the burial place of the Prophet Muhammad. A Muslim can perform the prayers anywhere, of course, if they cannot get to a mosque. Prayers are performed five times a day among Sunni Muslims: dawn, noon, afternoon, evening, and night. Shiite Muslims, like my grandmother, pray three times a day, combining the noon and afternoon prayers, as well as the evening and night prayers. Iran has the largest population of Shiites in the world, with almost 95% of its population adhering to Shiite Islam.

Like most Iranian men, Dad was an authoritarian. Although he never actually uttered the words, we knew we were loved. Unfortunately, in an Iranian household in the 1960s, a father who expressed such a sentiment was seen as "weak."

There were many mouths to feed and many problems to address. My father's occasional temper was aggravated by long workdays and his limited income. We learned to steer clear if Dad was tired or in a dark mood.

On one occasion, my brother Mohammad was crying through the night. The thin walls of our cramped duplex failed to block the baby's wails from entering my parents' room. My dad, upset about losing sleep before his next day of work, stormed into the living room where the children slept on the floor. He picked up Mohammad's crib and took it to the snow-covered balcony—with my crying brother still in it. He set the crib down, came back inside, and closed the door.

"Cry all you want!" he shouted. "I don't care. I need to get some sleep." With that, he trudged back to his bedroom and slammed the door. Of course, my mother and grandmother brought Mohammad inside within just a few minutes. The experience must have shocked my brother, however. He settled down for the rest of the night.

By the time I was 10, my dad and his business partner had expanded their shop, selling rice, teas, and dried vegetables to small delis throughout

Tehran. They would buy, for example, five 15 pounds bags of rice at each from the local farmer. Then, they would divide the rice and sell it in one-pound bags.

Nearly everyone sold some sort of food or merchandise at the local bazaar. My dad's leased shop was located along a strip of other stores. He was a shrewd businessman. With an education and opportunity, he could have done extremely well for himself.

However, education, as important as it is, has nothing to do with innate intelligence. What my dad lacked in education, he made up for with intelligence, an ability to understand human nature, and a natural sales mindset. He was, in fact, the best salesman I've ever met.

I learned one of my earliest business lessons from watching him handle customers—listening to understand their needs and treating them with respect. He focused on developing a strong rapport, particularly with his repeat customers. He knew them all by their first names and always asked about their families before handling business.

In the shop, my dad used a rudimentary abacus. I was amazed at how quickly and deftly his hands moved the beads along the frame's wires as he totaled the customer's purchase. While he was skilled with the abacus, he also partnered with someone who could read and write, trusting them to keep the books while Dad would handle the customers in the bazaar.

Unfortunately, it's important to remember that not everyone is honest.

One of Dad's partners, Mr. Zaferaian, was pocketing a serious amount of cash owed to the farmers in exchange for their goods. One day, the farmers came into the shop, demanding several months' worth of pay—nearly US$2,000 (equivalent to US$20,000 today). Imagine my father's shock and chagrin. Coincidentally, both Mr. Zaferaian and the money were nowhere to be found. As an equal partner in the shop, the farmers held my father accountable. With no money to give them, Dad spent two months in jail before being bailed out by a friend. After this experience, my dad would recite the old Iranian expression, "If the idea of having a business partner was a good idea, then God would have one!"

To a motivated (and innocent) businessman, such a situation could produce embarrassment and righteous anger. My dad also viewed it as a dire threat to his family as it stripped away our income and smeared his name. Thankfully, Dad was able to regain the trust of the people.

Growing up in Iran, it was not customary to celebrate birthdays. Today, however, sweets and cakes are enjoyed, but alcohol is not served due to Islamic laws. And although the celebrant will say they don't expect or want gifts, one should never believe them.

The most common birthday song was created in the 1960s by Iran Khodro, the manufacturer of the Paykan (which translates to arrow) automobile, a licensed version of the British Rootes Arrow popular in Iran for several decades. In Farsi, the song goes like this:

    Tavallod, Tavallod

Tavallodet mobārak

Mobārak mobārak

Tavallodet mobaarak

Labet shād o dele khosh, cho gol por khande bāshi

Biyā shamāro foot kon, ke sad sāl zende bāshi

Translated, it is:

    Birthday, birthday

Happy birthday

Happy happy

Happy birthday

May your lips be happy and your heart joyful,

and be always laughing like a flower.

Come on, blow the candles. May you live to be 100 years.

In 2002, my father visited me in the United States for my birthday. As we sat talking in the living room, eating the cake that my first wife, Rachel, had baked, I noticed a devilish glint in my father's eye.

"Why are you smiling like that?" I asked.

"Like what?" he said, still grinning. Although now in his 60s, my dad's dark eyes still sparkled with vitality, yet the lines around them spoke of the wisdom they held.

"Like the cat that ate the canary."

"Can't a father enjoy his son's birthday?"

"Yes, of course. But I know that look. I know you have something up your sleeve."

"Well," he said, putting his fork down and wiping his mouth with a napkin, "it turns out I do have something special for you on this birthday."

"I told you I don't need any gift from you. Simply coming to the States for my birthday celebration is such a beautiful gift."

"Well," he said, "this gift … it cost me nothing. Not even any wrapping paper. You see, it is not a gift that you open."

I finished my cake and leaned forward in my chair. "It sounds like quite the riddle," I said. "A gift that cost nothing and that I do not open. The suspense is killing me. What is it?"

He chuckled softly. "Well, son, you remember how I always told you and your brothers and sister how important it was to get an education? How I always stressed doing well in school?"

I laughed. "How could I forget?" Thoughts of that used blue bike in that long-ago shop in Tehran came to mind, but I didn't mention it. "We heard it all the time. 'Study, study, study. You don't know how lucky you are to be in school.'"

"Yes. Well, for me, I was anxious for you to start school. But, back in those days, you couldn't start public elementary school until you were seven years old. Seven! That's ridiculous. Nowadays, kids start at age six, like they do here in America. It's the right age to start."

"Okay," I said, still unsure where this was going. Was he going to give me some sort of award that I was supposed to have received in school? That seemed unlikely. "What's that have to do with my gift?"

He chuckled again, merriment dancing in his eyes. "Well, my son, today is your birthday, right?"

"That's what it says on my driver's license. Are you here to tell me differently?"

"I am here to tell you that the birth year on your passport and driver's license is incorrect. Those documents say 1951. You, son, were born in 1952. I'm giving you the gift of an extra year!" With that, he laughed and slapped his knee.

"What?" I was dumbfounded. "What are you talking about?"

"I told you I was impatient for you to start school. And to wait until age seven was not right. You needed to be in school at age six. I worked with government officials to change your birth certificate so that you could enter school a year earlier than you were allowed."

My jaw dropped open. "Are you kidding me?"

He smiled slyly. "It's amazing what a basket of fresh fruits and vegetables can do. Especially if offered to someone who must have been very hungry at the time."

We both laughed. Then, we stood and embraced.

"Thanks, Dad! I might be the only person in the world who just got younger on his birthday!"

In the entertainment industry, many people are known only by one name. Oprah. Cher. Bono. Eminem. Madonna. The list goes on.

In Iran, you didn't have to be in the entertainment industry or famous to go by one name. In fact, prior to 1919, Iranians didn't use surnames. After a government act introduced their use in 1919, the practice gained traction during the reign of Reza Shah (1925-1941), who made surnames mandatory. Prior to the rule, a combination of prefixes and suffixes attached to a name would distinguish one person from the next. People were often known by the name of the district or town they came from, attaching the locality's name as a suffix. For example, Khorasani signified that a person came from the Khorasan Province, Gilani was linked to the Gilan Province, and Tehrani indicated a person was from Tehran.

Once the mandate was proclaimed, my father joined the thousands of others without a surname who began to flood into government offices across the country. I imagine there were plenty of government officials who went home tired, muttering dark sentiments against Reza Shah (but first making sure they were out of the earshot of others – they dared not speak out against such authority). Iran in the 1940s was hardly like America in the 21st century, where presidents and other leaders can be mocked and made the subject of mean-spirited, albeit humorous, jokes.

As my father related the story, he walked into the center of Langarood, taking his place in a slow-moving line of people with only one name. They shuffled one by one into a tent set up by the government to document last names. The air was thick with humidity; the people sweltered in the heat. By the time my father approached the cardboard table inside the tent, his cheeks were red. A small fan blew hot air around the two seated officials.

"Do you have a last name?" asked an official.

"No, sir. That is why I am here," my father replied.

"Very well. We'll assign you one. Do you have one in mind?"

He had thought they'd just give him a name. "No."

The second official looked at his colleague with a sly grin. "Look at his cheeks," he said. "Why don't we call him Khone Kaboter?"

"Khone Kaboter?" my father asked. It translated to Blood of Pigeon.

"Yeah. It'll make you stand out. That's what a last name is supposed to do."

To be honest, my father later told me that he didn't care what name he was assigned. It wouldn't make a difference to his life in the small village of Langarood.

"Fine," he said. The officials issued him a certificate that declared his new name: Gholam Hussein Khone Kaboter.

When I was born, I became Mehdi Blood of Pigeon.

When I was eight years old, the other children at my all-boys school (segregation by gender is still practiced in Iranian schools today) began to tease me about my odd last name and my Gilaki accent.

"Blood of Pigeon!" they taunted. "I bet I know what you had for dinner last night! Pigeon!"

"Yeah, he has blood all over his lips!"

"I wondered why he has a feather in his hair!"

After school, I was careful to wipe the tears from my face before my father could say, "Big boys don't cry."

My brothers and I faced teasing and torment for weeks. One afternoon, I finally begged him to change our last name.

"What are you talking about?"

"The kids at school are making fun of us! All the time!"

He shook his head and told us not to listen to those children. Toughen up.

"Learning to take their taunts will make you stronger," he said. But I didn't want to be stronger. I wanted to fit in.

Finally, perhaps just so we'd stop pestering him, Dad headed to the government office to begin the paperwork to change our name. We cheered. Then, a dreadful thought crept over me. What if he made a simple change like Blood of Hawk or Blood of Crow? Hours passed before we saw him walking up the road toward home.

"Did you change it?" I asked with great trepidation.

"I did," he smiled.

"To what?" I was ready to stow away on a passenger ship if the name was blood of anything.

"To Khosrow-Pour," he said.

"Khosrow-Pour?" I asked. "What does that mean?"

"It's good," he said, dismissing me with a wave of his hand. "Now, let me be. I'm tired and have done you a great favor."

I later found out that Khosrow means "king" or "ruler of dynasties." Pour means "first" and "most ancient." Mehdi means "rightly guided." Loosely translated, my name means "rightly guided ruler of an ancient and leading dynasty."

Not bad for a kid who was born and raised in poverty.

Oh, my classmate tormentors? They quieted down once they heard my new last name.

Chapter 3
Pushing the Boulder

If having an embarrassing last name was the only trauma I went through in my childhood, I'd be a lucky man indeed. Of course, however, every person experiences trauma and tragedy in their life.

I will say that many of my early childhood memories are a bit blurry, directly due to of a few traumatic events. It's likely that I suffer from dissociative amnesia, which is a condition where you block out certain events in your life because they are too painful to remember. It's the brain's way of protecting you from further harm.

At any rate, my first major trauma occurred when I was about 11 years old. I remember coming home from school and joining a group of kids near my home in a game of soccer. A close friend of mine was in this group, and he came up to me.

"Mehdi, what are you doing here?"

"What do you mean?" I replied. "I'm playing soccer, just like you are."

"Didn't you hear about your mother?"

"My mother? What about her?"

He looked at me very solemnly for a moment. "Mehdi, she died. Just this afternoon. You should go home."

I looked at him curiously, feeling a sinking sensation in my heart. I wasn't certain what death was, but he clearly wasn't relaying good news. I ran home and entered our house to find my grandmother and my siblings all crying. Even my father was crying. I had never seen him cry before this (in fact, he always reminded us that "big boys don't cry").

My grandmother was with her daughter—my mother was now the fifth and final child that my grandmother had lost—and when she saw me come into the room, she beckoned me to come and held me in her arms. I could feel her warm tears on my face. When I looked at my mother lying there, I understood what death was. She was not sleeping, not resting. She was gone. Forever.

I began weeping too.

My mother was only 33 years old when she passed away. So young! She had lived a challenging life: marrying at 13, giving birth to seven children in quick succession, and living in poor conditions. These all added to the stressors of her life, but what likely killed her was a genetic blood disorder called glucose-6-phosphate dehydrogenase deficiency (G6PD). This disorder disproportionately affects people throughout the Mediterranean and Middle East. G6PD results in the destruction of red blood cells in response to an illness, certain medications, or even foods like lima beans. Some people, including myself, are passive and asymptomatic carriers of the disease. In fact, G6PD doesn't affect me at all. My mother was not so lucky. Oddly enough, it is men who normally have this deficiency; it is rare in women.

Further hampering my mother's health was the misdiagnosis of her condition. The doctor she saw was convinced it was jaundice and treated her for that condition. However, her symptoms were more severe, most likely requiring a blood transfusion, oxygen, and intravenous fluids. The mistake is understandable because G6PD symptoms include fatigue and yellowed skin, which are also symptoms of jaundice.

I have few specific memories of my mother. I do remember her warmth and love for her children. But losing her at such a tender age, and with my memory hampered by dissociative amnesia, I remember little else about her.

My dad became a widower at 34. He greatly loved my mother and mourned her loss, which caused him to spiral. He had five kids to take care of, and his business to tend to—a business that he had built into a decently successful venture. Still, he was adrift, unfocused, unable to concentrate or be in the moment. In a way, it reminds me of Sisyphus, the king of Ephyra in Greek mythology. Dad was forced to push an immense boulder up a hill, only for it to roll down each time it neared the top. Sisyphus had to repeat this action for eternity as punishment for cheating death twice. And now here was my father, who had built a solid business out of nothing, only to see it begin to falter and collapse when his shady business partner, Mr. Zaferaian, made off with the money owed to the farmers. My dad pushed that boulder all the way up the hill–only to see it fall back down.

Ironically, my father had not cheated death, as in the case of Sisyphus; death had cheated him. Then, his business partner cheated on him as well, leaving my father to face the consequences. After his two months in jail for Mr. Zaferaian's crime, Dad lost his business and was forced to sell our house.

By this time, Dad had remarried; this was two years after my mother's death. His second wife, Haj Khonoom, was three years his senior and the daughter of one of the country's early ayatollahs. She also had a daughter from her previous marriage. An extremely religious woman, she wore a black hijab that covered all but her eyes when she went out.

I was 14 when we moved into the second story of my stepmother's home in central Tehran. There were 15 people living in the house, including two of Haj Khonoom's two sisters and their families.

My dad, my stepmother, my grandmother, my siblings and I lived on the second floor, which had four tiny bedrooms. The house had no indoor bathroom. Instead, there was an outhouse in the backyard, which all 15 of us had to share. I remember shuffling through the snow to go to the bathroom on cold winter nights! There was no heating or air conditioning (which was equally needed in the hot summers). Although the bathroom had running water, it would often freeze in the coldest months, forcing us to take a pitcher of water with us from inside the house because the tap water was frozen.

My dad began working at the shop of another business owner. He was now responsible for feeding nine mouths. He worked ungodly hours to do so—sometimes up to 80 or 90 hours a week. During this period, we barely saw him; he was almost always at the shop.

Another change that took place after my mom died was that my dad—in great part because he was hardly ever home—instructed Ali, who was seven years older than me, to be the disciplinarian while he was at the shop. On the surface, this made a lot of sense. Naturally, the oldest child would assume the leadership role in the house while Dad was gone. That was all very understandable and normal.

Unfortunately, my brother took his role as the older brother in charge of disciplining us to the extreme. He was very abusive; there were times that he beat us with his belt for little mistakes that we made or if our homework was not done 100% correctly. He physically abused me and my other siblings. Instead of being a pillar of support after our mother's death, Ali betrayed my father's trust. And we all paid the price.

I started experiencing severe migraines. Like a shield, I began feeling a sense of detachment from my emotions and gaps in my memory. The abuse happened on a regular basis, and it's another reason that this period of my life is largely a blur because of the dissociative amnesia that I experienced. The amnesia acted like a protective covering over me, shielding me from further harm.

My dad had no idea this abuse was happening – and we never told him. Partly, I didn't want to add stress to my dad's life, which already had enough stress in it. He always thought I was a happy boy, and I didn't want to mar that image. So, I suffered through that trauma alone.

In just a few short years, I had lost both my mom and our home, faced physical abuse from my brother, and suffered through severe migraines. I began to give into feelings of deep despair. Life became bleak. I fought against the depression that was enshrouding me. My dreams of getting a topnotch education and a fulfilling career and life slipped further and further away. Who was I kidding? I was a poor kid without a mother. My living conditions in my stepmother's house were less than ideal. My brother was abusive, and my father was hardly ever there (or distracted when he was around). My life was miserable at that moment, and I sometimes had a hard time seeing it getting better. For the first time, I began to understand why people commit suicide. There were times when I contemplated it myself. It would end my misery. The pain of everything, particularly the migraine headaches, would disappear. Just when I'd get rid of one migraine and feel the immense relief of not having that searing pain in my head, another would come on. They were relentless. The kind of life I was living didn't seem, at times, worth living.

Thankfully, I never acted on those impulses. I kept trudging on, kept moving forward day by day, step by step. Just like my father – even like Sisyphus. Again. And again. I felt like I was forever pushing that boulder, having it come crashing back down on me, getting to my feet again, pushing it up that hill. Always with the small and indomitable hope that could not be snuffed out in me: I will make it. My life will get better. I will realize my dreams.

Maybe not today, maybe not tomorrow. But some day.

And that hope kept me going.

As we settled into our new life in my stepmother's house, I noticed two things. First, my stepmother seemed to resent my dad's five kids. She clearly favored her biological daughter and the children—two girls and a boy—that she had over us. This isn't that unusual in mixed families, and I can't blame her for that. She now had so many kids—not even biologically hers—to care for. Although many of my biological siblings didn't much care for our stepmother, I actually liked her and could understand what was going on. I went out of my way to help her feel like she was a genuine part of our larger family. In my role as peacekeeper, I helped her out around the house when she asked.

Second, my father acted differently around Haj Khonoom than he did around my mother. It's a simple fact – you can't force love or other feelings. I'm sure my father loved his new wife. Still, it was not at all in the way he loved my biological mother. My mother was the love of his life. No one could replace her. He had brought love, passion, hopes, and dreams to his first marriage. To this new marriage, he brought the ability to provide for a woman and her child in exchange for her ability to care for his children and keep their home. It was a marriage of arrangement, not of the heart.

Haj Khonoom recognized this, causing resentment between them.

That resentment was fueled by my father's Friday morning routine of traveling 15 miles to visit my mother's grave. Sometimes, he would take us. I remember watching him sob at my mother's graveside. Even as the years passed, he missed her so much. He could not get over the loss, refusing to give up her memory. This infuriated his new wife.

He had married my mother when he was a teen. Together, they'd had seven children. They'd weathered good times and bad times together. They had traversed their teenage years and early adulthood years together, experiencing many changes in their lives and so many ups and downs. To his first marriage, he had brought love, hope, and dreams. It is, therefore, not hard to understand his feelings for my mother.

He was a very different man when he married Haj Khonoom. He was world wise and world-weary. He had built his own successful business and worked himself to the bone to give us a better life than he had. He was not that starstruck young lover that he was at age 14.

This chapter is titled "Pushing the Boulder" for good reason: Our lives were a series of struggles reminiscent of Sisyphus's punishment of eternally pushing that boulder uphill. But not everything was an uphill battle.

My dad, who had been forced to sell his business when his partner scammed him and the farmers they bought goods from and who had been working for someone else in the convening two years, finally saved up enough money to lease a very small shop and start a new business for himself similar to the one he had previously owned. This time, he hired my sister's husband, Ali, to run the books for him. Ali was already doing this sort of work for another business. My dad's new shop was very small, about six feet by 10 feet, tucked around a corner underneath a staircase. He was once again his own boss. His prior customers returned, as did the sparkle in his eyes.

Mohammad and I would help him in the shop. We'd watch Dad make shrewd decisions and negotiations, much like a person with multiple degrees. We enjoyed this role because we saw Dad thrive. He seemed to understand the psychology of both the sales business and how to handle customers. One time, only half-jokingly, my father nudged me as a man approached with a wad of rials in his pocket.

"You see that money? It's my job to make sure he spends all of it in my shop." Dad could maximize every sale while simultaneously making his customers feel welcomed, respected, and happy.

Sometimes, you get a job because you know the right person. And sometimes you get a job because the right person gets arrested.

I got one of my more memorable early jobs the latter way.

It all started with the arrest of a tenant, Amir Karimi, who rented a room in my stepmother's house for himself, his wife, and their two children. He worked in a very classy antique shop in a nice neighborhood in north-central Tehran. It was miles away from our southcentral neighborhood – and a world away from our socioeconomic conditions. This shop sold beautiful Persian rugs, French crystal, bronze statues, and great paintings, with many items priced at US$10,000 or more.

One evening, we heard a loud banging on our door. My stepmother, wearing her indoor hijab, which covered her head and shoulders but not her face (not her less-revealing hijab, as she was not outdoors) opened the door and stood back in alarm. Three men—two of them police officers—were looking at her. I'm sure she was dismayed to have any man other than my dad see her face.

"We're looking for Amir Karimi!" one of the officers barked.

"Yes, yes. Just a moment," she replied, hurrying to the basement where the Karimi family had their room. Within a few minutes, she came back up the stairs with Mr. Karimi, who frowned and was hesitant to look the officers in the face.

"You are Amir Karimi?" the first officer asked.

"Yes, sir."

"That's him, all right," said the man who had accompanied the officers.

"You work at this man's shop, the Javadi Antique Shop on Naderi Avenue?" The first officer pointed toward the man standing behind him.

Mr. Karimi nodded, the look on his face becoming guiltier by the moment.

"How could you steal from me?" the man, apparently Mr. Javadi, asked. "You betrayed my trust. I give you work, and you steal from me!"

Mr. Karimi looked like he was about to offer a weak denial, but the first officer cut him short. "Show me your room," the officer demanded.

Mr. Karimi looked abjectly at my stepmother, who stepped aside to allow the three men to follow Mr. Karimi to the basement. They soon returned, with Mr. Javadi carrying a statuette and a box with four very valuable Baccarat crystal glasses.

While that was the last time we saw Mr. Karimi, it was not the last we saw of the shopkeeper, Mr. Javadi. My father, never one to miss an opportunity, had come downstairs when he heard the commotion of the arrest, never one to miss an opportunity. He approached Mr. Javadi.

He introduced himself. "You own an antique shop on Naderi Avenue?"

Mr. Javadi nodded. "One of the finest antique shops in Tehran."

My father smiled appreciatively. "I am sure it is. And now you have lost an employee." He stroked his chin for a moment. "Tell me, do you need another employee to help you in the shop?"

"I do," Mr. Javadi grumbled. "Amir has left me short-handed. Are you looking for work?"

"Well, I'm not looking for work. I own my own shop as well. But my son is 14. He's very dependable, very reliable," he said, motioning at me. "And very honest," my dad added, knowing that was now a sore spot with Mr. Javadi.

As the shopkeeper sized me up, I tried my best to look dependable, reliable, and honest. Apparently, I succeeded. Mr. Javadi, with a small grin on his face, asked my name.

"Mehdi."

His eyebrows shot up. "Mehdi! That is also my name." He smiled at me. "Well, Mehdi, would you like to work for me this summer?"

My eyes lit up. A fancy store in one of the nicest sections of the city?

"Yes, sir," I said. "Very much so."

Mr. Javadi gave me a business card with the shop's address. "You show up tomorrow and I'll put you to work."

"Yes, sir!" I replied.

To get to the Javadi Antique Shop, I had to get up quite early and take two city buses. Relying on buses was new for me, as I had always been able to walk nearly everywhere I needed to go. I felt grown up, commuting with other workers as we rolled through the streets of Tehran. My excitement grew as the streets became cleaner and wider. The stores turned into buildings, and the buildings turned into skyscrapers. I was seeing a part of Tehran that I rarely saw. At the raw age of 14, my eyes were wide open in wonder.

I was amazed to see all the beautiful and expensive items at the antique shop. I was nervous about walking around, afraid I would knock something off a shelf and break it. If I did, we'd be in debt for the rest of our lives! But I didn't break anything, and Mr. Javadi was very kind to me as he showed me around and put me to work.

The work was far from glamorous—vacuuming, sweeping, and washing the tiled portion of the floor, cleaning the store's front window and the bathroom, bringing tea to customers, and carrying purchases to customers' cars. Still, it was new and exciting to me.

It gave me a greater appreciation for the various types and levels of business. With just one sale, the antique store could bring in more money than my father's business might make in one year. Mr. Javadi and my father were both businessmen, but the world in which Mr. Javadi operated was vastly different from my dad's.

In fact, it made me appreciate my father for being a part of the business world—an entrepreneur. Dad was making things happen in his world to the very best of his limited opportunities. Mr. Javadi, on the other hand, had many more opportunities as an entrepreneur. He, too, was making the most of them.

I realized that I could also make something of myself. All I needed was to position myself where my opportunities were the greatest. That would be the foundation upon which I would build.

I worked quite happily for Mr. Javadi, taking the bus to and from his shop, exchanging my poor neighborhood for his rich neighborhood. I watched as he conducted business with wealthy clients, each day soaking in a bit more real-world education and restoring my dreams of becoming a successful businessman. A man like Mr. Javadi. And, yes, like my father too.

Chapter 4
Swimming Upstream

I assumed, in the summer that I worked in Mr. Javadi's shop, that my work would be over when school began. I was looking forward to starting ninth grade. Just as it is in America, going from eighth grade to ninth grade in those days was a milestone, serving as the midpoint of a student's six-year high school education in Iran. Every student had to select one of the three major areas of study—biology, math, or literature—for the rest of their high school years.

During the summer, I made 180 tomans per month, worth US$25 in those days, which was decent money for a kid at that time. I was grateful for the job. I really liked Mr. Javadi, and it made me feel a bit grown up to be working in his shop and making money on my own. Dad, however, was struggling financially at the time. So, each month I gave 100 tomans from my earnings to help our family. Of course, I would have liked to have kept the money for myself. Still, I respected my father, knowing how hard he worked. I knew that his opportunities to make decent money were limited without an education. I was also happy to be able to contribute to the family's needs. After all, Dad had sacrificed everything he had to provide for us my whole life.

Still, you can imagine my surprise when Dad sat me down in our living room not long before school was to begin again. He looked somber and serious.

"Mehdi, you are not going to be able to go back to school. We need the extra income that you are making."

I sat there, stunned. My mind feverishly worked for a way out. I wanted to continue my education. I needed to. I loved my father, but I didn't want to turn out like him. His illiteracy and lack of education were like a prison—it was a very dim future indeed.

"Maybe I could go to school and work too," I said. "Maybe Mr. Javadi would let me come to work after school."

"No!" he said, his brow furrowing and his eyes darkening. "Even if he would allow that, part-time work is not enough. We need the income from full-time work. You need to continue full-time at the shop."

With that, he stood up and walked out of the living room, his stride tense and swift. Perhaps he was angry with me for my suggestion. His decree, after all, was the law in our house. But now, looking back, I believe he was angry with the situation, upset that I had to work and sacrifice my dreams of getting not just a high school education, but also a college degree.

He knew he was taking my dream from me. And he hated that.

At the time, I didn't see that. All I saw was that I was going the route of so many Iranian youths—dropping out of school to work. (In Iran, the literacy rate was 36% in 1976; by 2021, that rate had risen to 89%.) I was destined to be a dropout with a dead-end job.

The perception of my beloved summer job at the Javadi Antique Shop quickly dimmed. Instead, my work felt menial. I swallowed my resentment as I served the rich customers. I tried to hold back my frustration and bitterness at not continuing school.

Unbeknownst to me, Dad had apparently already talked to Mr. Javadi about me staying on full-time after the summer. Just after I spoke to my father, Mr. Javadi said he was glad I would be staying at the shop.

"I need good workers like you, Mehdi," Mr. Javadi said as I swept the store's floor one afternoon. I could tell he was trying to be nice to me; he knew I wanted to return to school. I glumly nodded at him and continued sweeping.

It was hard not to be bitter. I had to give up school for this menial job, yet I wasn't even old enough to cash my paychecks at a bank. To open a bank account, I had to alter the year of my birthday on my local library card, which had my picture on it. And remember, my father had already made me one year older than I really was. So, with this alteration, I was now two years older than my true age. Though I was only 14, according to my card, I was 16. Because of that, I was able to open an account to deposit my money.

So, as all of the kids in my neighborhood and my former classmates returned to school, I kept taking the two buses to the Javadi Antique Shop, where I continued to sweep and clean and carry out rugs and other items purchased by customers, putting the items in their late-model cars.

My coworkers, several men who were more than a decade my senior, lacked motivation. Many of them had been working in the shop for 10 or 15 years. They had purposeless lives. After work, they went to the local teahouse, smoking hookah over the same tired jokes. Eventually, they'd head to their homes for their dinners before going to bed as they prepared to do it all over again the next day—endlessly repeating a dull life. Their outlook on life was dismal.

And their monotonous routine was the life I appeared destined to live. The thought of waking up every day to do the same unfulfilling tasks was daunting. I craved meaning, excitement, and purpose.

After a few months of sulking and moping, I made a decision that changed my destiny.

We all have choices to make in life. Sometimes, those choices affect our life's trajectory in small ways. At other times, they set in motion what essentially is a whole new life from the one you were living and would have continued to live had you not made that choice. Hollywood, for example, has made a number of movies based on how one small decision can change the course of a person's life (like Forrest Gump or It's a Wonderful Life).

So, it was with my life.

After a year of working at Mr. Javadi's antique shop (and losing one year of going to school), I decided to simultaneously work my full-time job and continue my education by registering for preparation night school.

The education systems in Iran and America differed in many ways during the 1960s. For instance, America offered a one-time general educational development (GED) test covering language arts, math, social studies, and science. Once the student passes the test, they earn a high school equivalency diploma. In Iran, however, dropout students were required to sit out an entire year before taking tests for each year missed. This meant I would have to take separate tests to prove I had the knowledge to pass 9th, 10th, 11th, and 12th grades. These policies were designed to discourage students from dropping out. Subjects included science, social studies, geography, math, biology, chemistry, physics, and a foreign language.

I worked at the antique shop from seven in the morning until seven at night. During my 30-minute lunchbreak at the store, I'd hustle over to a local deli to order a baguette lathered in butter and jam. Every so often, on special occasions, I'd enjoy an apple with my lunch.

My salary had increased to 6.50 tomans a day, and I was averaging an extra 20 tomans in tips each month for ferrying antiques. Tuition cost 60 tomans a month, and I was still contributing 100 tomans a month—the lion's share of my earnings—to help support our family. After working my 12-hour shift, I'd commute on my bike across town to begin night school at 7:30 p.m., preparing for the GED.

All in all, I was eking out a barebones living.

By the time I was 15, I had scrounged up enough loose change to buy what I had dreamt of buying three years earlier: my bicycle. The circumstances of the purchase were vastly different from the near purchase when I was 12.

I went—this time on my own—to a used bike shop in my neighborhood. It was a different shop from the one my father took me to three years earlier (the one where I had been so close to getting that snazzy blue bike but blew it when I told my dad the shopkeeper's asking price was fair). This shop was a little bigger and had more selection. The owner, a much younger man in his 30s, eyed me dully.

"Salam," he greeted me with little enthusiasm. He likely thought a kid on his own was not going to buy a bike.

As I looked around the shop, the man came up to me, striking up a conversation (probably out of boredom).

"What kind of bike are you looking for?"

"Something sturdy," I said. "Something I can rely on."

He appraised me curiously; most boys wanted something sleek and flashy, which is what I'd yearned for three years ago. But my needs had changed. Now, I was looking for a reliable bike, one that could get me back and forth from home to work, to night school and back home again. No breakdowns. No flat tires.

The salesman showed me three different used bikes that, according to him, were "quite sturdy." I gave them test rides. The first had stiff gears and was clumsy. The second's front tire wobbled a bit. The third one, however, was a smooth ride, shifted cleanly, had newer tires with good tread on them, and had a greased chain. Its seat was worn but comfortable.

"I like this one," I said, returning from my test ride. "How much is it?"

The man, still eyeing me curiously (probably asking himself if "this kid" was actually going to buy a bike), told me the cost, confident I would just accept his asking price. But I was older and wiser than three years earlier, and I had learned a lot about bartering from my father and Mr. Javadi. I countered, and we went back and forth before settling on a price.

I rode home on the bike I'd bought with my own money. The bike I'd haggled for with my own wits and appraised with my own eyes for its durability. I couldn't help but grin. The breeze on my face felt wonderful—like I was flying—as I passed by the little shops and the one-story houses attached to each other in our neighborhood.

I finally had my own bike. I had bought it on my own terms. And the road ahead was wide open.

I cherished that bike as much as many people in America treasure the purchase of their first used car. It opened a new world for me, giving me mobility and a sense of independence. My next purchase was a sturdy lock with a thick bolt—I couldn't afford to have the lock cut and my bike stolen!

Even with the thick lock, I kept a nervous eye on the bike throughout my workday at the antique shop. Once my day was over, I'd hop on the bike and ride the 20 minutes to school. When the evening's session was over at 10:30 p.m., I'd ride in the dark to my friend Hussein's house, 10 minutes from the school. Hussein and I became fast friends during night school. We hit it off immediately. He was a bit overweight and was always telling jokes, which made him fun to be around. Like me, he'd lost a parent—his father—when he was five years old. Now, Hussein and his two older brothers worked to support his mother and two younger sisters.

We'd study at his house, sometimes until the early hours of the morning. We were both motivated to get through high school, to better our lives. It was a lesson in teamwork—if one was strong, two were stronger. We'd test our knowledge by answering the questions, solving the problems, and comparing our answers to the correct answers in the back of the book. We had a common goal, and it's sometimes easier to work toward a goal when you are working in concert with someone.

The result of the impending GED lingered in my mind throughout the day, like a shadow I couldn't escape. If I passed, I would move on to the next level. A failing grade meant I'd start all over again.

I never saw Hussein's mother. Being very religious, she did not want to show herself to a male outside of her family. Often, she would knock on the door of the living room where we studied, offering us tea, nuts, or figs. We'd thank her and give her a moment to retreat before opening the door to enjoy our snacks. Once, I caught the briefest glance of her floor-length dress as she rounded a corner.

Tehran, situated on the slopes of the Alborz Mountains, is nearly 3,000 feet above sea level. The weather is not much different from New York

City, although many people assume it is always hot. Tehran has cold winters, sometimes snowing up to three feet. There were nights when I had to carefully maneuver my bike through snowy, slushy, icy streets after studying with Hussein. I'd try to avoid traffic and stay upright. I'd navigate my way through the labyrinth of the Grand Bazaar and its maze of seemingly endless covered stalls, an icy wind cutting straight through me, freezing my face and hands. When I would arrive home, my face and hands were always red; sometimes I was so cold that I could barely move my facial muscles to talk normally.

My grandmother, bless her, would always be waiting for me with a cup of hot tea, no matter what time I finally made it home.

"You don't have to wait up, Grandma," I'd say, though it made me feel good.

"You know I cannot sleep until I know we are all safe and sound," she'd reply, warming my hands by rubbing them between her own while we waited for the water to boil. "I wish you didn't have to be out so late. I worry about a boy your age not being with his family. But I know you are trying hard to complete your education, and that is admirable."

She would talk quietly, not wanting to wake my two younger brothers, Mohammad and Ahmad. Our household had become quite crowded.

I'd drink my tea, and we'd go to bed—my grandmother, my two younger brothers, and I sharing a twin mattress on the den's hard floor. We were like Russian nesting dolls, each person smaller than the next. The room's single kerosene lamp did little to heat the room. It wasn't very comfortable, but in the winter, the added body heat helped fend off the cold winter nights.

Those cold winter trips between home, work, and school were made bearable by the compassion of Mr. Davoodi, one of Mr. Javadi's most loyal customers. Mr. Davoodi was a Jewish lawyer who led a prestigious law firm in Tehran. One winter day, as I carried a set of expensive French bronze statuettes that Mr. Davoodi had purchased for his home, he stopped and looked at me after opening the trunk of what looked like a brand-new (and spotless) luxury Mercedes Benz.

"Mehdi, why didn't you put your coat on? It's freezing." Mr. Davoodi gave me a kind but concerned smile.

I lowered my head, embarrassed that I didn't have a winter coat. Instead, I was wearing two sweaters.

"It's okay, Mr. Davoodi. I'm not cold," I said, my teeth chattering.

He slowly shook his head, furrowed his brow, and snorted in disbelief. A trail of my foggy breath was whisked away by the sharp wind. I carefully set the statuettes, wrapped in bubble wrap and snug in a box, in his trunk. He closed the trunk and looked at me again.

"Nonsense," he said. "I can see that you're shivering. Hold on a moment." He reached inside his fur coat, pulling 100 tomans from the wallet inside his pocket.

"Take this," Mr. Davoodi said. "Go out today and buy yourself a nice warm coat. You understand?"

I looked at him, startled, and took the money. "Th-thank you, sir," I said, stumbling over my words, partly because I was overwhelmed by his generosity and partly because I was so cold.

The next day, I visited a local shop that sold long winter coats, luxuriating in their weight and fabrics. It was the same feeling I experienced when I first set my eyes on the blue Schwinn that I so desperately wanted at age 12. I'd never imagined I would have such a warm winter coat, at least not at my age and under my circumstances.

I selected a long coat with a warm lining. Its original cost was 100 tomans, exactly what Mr. Asher had given me. I, however, managed to talk the owner down to 85 tomans.

A few days later, Mr. Davoodi returned to the antique shop. This was surprising because he often went for a few months between visits. He was not shopping for antiques; he had come to see if I'd bought a coat. When I spotted him, I rushed to the storage room to retrieve it.

"Let me see you try it on," he said, grinning. He said I looked great in it and that he was happy I had bought it.

I'd kept the remaining 15 tomans in my pocket. Although I could think of a dozen ways to spend the money, I was determined to return it to Mr. Davoodi, repaying kindness with kindness. I extended my hand with the money, explaining what it was.

"No, Mehdi, you keep that," he shook his head and smiled. "Spend it however you want. I'm just glad you got the coat." With that, he turned and left the store.

That coat got me through a lot of cold winter nights for many years. I'll never forget Mr. Davoodi's kindness, or the joy in his face when he saw my enthusiasm. I vowed that one day, I would pay it forward, ensuring that someone else experienced the same kindness and support.

Years later, I thought of Mr. Davoodi during a ride home from New York's Penn Station. A police officer stopped my taxi driver, accusing him of running a traffic light. The officer said he wasn't interested in my opinion when I spoke up for the driver, relaying that I didn't recall him running the light. The driver was issued a ticket for US$250.

As we continued our drive downtown, I could hear the driver telling his wife over the phone that he couldn't afford to pay for his ticket. After he ended his call, I started a conversation with him, learning that he and his six children had come to the United States from Haiti as refugees two years prior.

"I barely make 200 dollars on a 10-hour shift," he said, his voice breaking, "and now I have to pay a ticket I didn't deserve in the first place. It's not fair. But what can I do?" Through the rearview mirror, I saw tears of frustration and desperation in his eyes.

When we reached my apartment, the cab fare was US$20. I handed him US$270, telling him to use the extra money to pay for the ticket. His eyes grew very large when he saw all the money I handed him.

"Oh, no, sir, I cannot take all this money from you!" He was sniffling through his tears now.

"No, you're right," I said. "It wasn't fair. I have the money and you don't. So, you take this and let me help you out. It makes me happy to do so."

He looked at me. "You are giving me 250 extra dollars!" he said.

"I'm helping you out because I can," I replied. "And it makes me happy to do so."

He thanked me profusely. As I exited his cab, I thought of Mr. Davoodi giving me the money for my winter coat. It was then that I realized the joy that Mr. Davoodi must have derived from helping me out. When a random act of kindness is carried out, two people—the receiver and the giver—are blessed.

I felt a twinge of guilt when I showed up to school in my new coat. Many of my classmates were kids who were poorer than me. One kid worked full-time, commuting 90 miles back and forth to school on a moped. He'd travel along dark and dangerous roads, arriving at class with his ears and cheeks purple from the cold winter night.

Surrounded by kids in similar or worse situations, I began to take stock of my life. I'd been gifted a warm coat for the winter. I had a grandmother who loved me and doted on me. I knew my father loved me, though he'd never say so. There was a roof over my head and food to eat. I had a good, steady job with a respectable employer who liked me. Other than my migraines, I was in good health. Even if I did have to work all day, at least I had the opportunity to go to night school to advance my education, taking one measured step at a time toward my dream. I took pride in being a breadwinner for my family at age 15. My view of the world had greatly expanded as I better appreciated the lessons learned from the hardships of working long hours at a meager wage. I wasn't happy to experience them, but I learned some valuable lessons through them. I learned I was resilient, capable, and responsible. I learned I could overcome hardships.

Above all, I learned I could still dream. In fact, my dream of a better life just became stronger, sharper, more focused, and more tangible the more trials I went through in life.

As author and theologian Lewis B. Smedes said, "Hope is to our spirits what oxygen is to our lungs. Lose hope and you will die. They may not bury you for a while, but without hope you are dead inside."

I held on to hope. I cherished it, protected it, fed it, and watered it. I vowed that I would never let hope's light darken.

Night school was preparing me to walk confidently across the stepping stones into my future. Even with a full-time job, I was still a strong student. I had always done well in school, and I really applied myself to my studies. I was determined not to let my circumstances get in the way of my aspirations. That's why I studied so hard with Hussein.

Each spring for the next four years, I easily passed the GED and moved to the next level of night school. I continued to work at the antique shop, contributing to the family funds. I had grown and put on some weight; I had become a young man. The bike I'd bought carried me across my routine route for four years from home to work to school with only a few replaced tires. But it was more than worth it. That bike turned out to be one of the earliest vehicles for realizing my dream.

Finally, after earning my high school equivalency diploma at age 18, I was ready—and excited—for the next phase: university.

Maz Jobrani, an Iranian comedian and actor who moved to America with his parents when he was six, once said something along these lines: "Iranian parents tell their children they have three career options: become a medical doctor, an engineer, or a disgrace to the family."

Given those options, I chose medical doctor. For three years, I concentrated on biology courses to achieve my high school equivalency. The goal of becoming a medical doctor was the carrot in front of my nose, propelling me forward.

To be honest, simply earning my high school equivalency diploma ruled out the third option of being a disgrace to the family. My dad, never having gone to school, was proud of me for simply making it through high school, especially while I worked a full-time job. So, attaining that equivalency was the first, most straightforward step toward this goal.

After briefly celebrating my GED success, I buckled down to the task at hand: preparing for the dreaded Iranian University Entrance Exam (known as Konkour).

Konkour is a grueling exam that every student who wants to go on to higher education in Iran must take. The rigorous four-and-a-half-hour exam covers all subjects taught in Iranian high schools, from math and science to Islamic studies and foreign languages. Those who take the test normally spend years studying for it.

The competition for admission to Iranian higher education was, and continues to be, fierce. Today, more than 50% of applicants are admitted to public universities with free tuition in Iran. When I was applying, only about 3% were admitted. Most applicants came from upper-class or upper-middle-class families. With this exam, it was not only what you knew, but who you knew. And well-connected, wealthier parents would leverage their connections and status to get their children into a university of their choice.

Those types of shady dealings are not restricted to Iran. Later, when I served on a graduate selection committee, I would receive calls from the administration instructing me to prioritize certain applicants because their relatives were government officials or large donors to the university. And this wasn't just an issue at one American university. In 2019, more than 50 people were charged in an undergraduate admissions scandal at several top

American universities after it was learned that many of them paid bribes to have their children enrolled.

Well, my father was in no position to have such powerful connections! I knew, going in, that the odds were against me. However, this motivated me to study even harder. I registered for preparatory classes, bought study guides and copies of old tests, and threw myself into preparing for Konkour. I studied with Hussein for nine months before taking the exams.

On the morning of the first portion of the test, which was spread over two days, I ate a hurried breakfast, drank a bit of tea, and biked to the University of Tehran. I left the test tired, unable to think clearly as I eagerly put distance between myself and the testing site. I just needed to relax. At first, I found myself replaying many of the test questions in my head, wondering if I answered them correctly. That, however, only lasted a few minutes. Then, I let it go, thinking about anything but that day's test or the ones coming up tomorrow.

Within a few weeks of completing Konkour, I received my results in the mail. In Iran, students list their top 10 university choices and subjects of interest. My scores, however, wouldn't grant me admission to my first nine choices. I was bitterly disappointed. Still, I received an offer of admission for the second half of the year to the University of Tehran's School of Cinema and Dramatic Arts.

A tiny part of me wanted to accept that offer. It was, after all, an admittance to the university known as "The Mother University of Iran," one of the best universities in the Middle East. It is, indeed, among the top universities in the world. It would be very prestigious to be an alumnus of the university.

While I appreciate cinema and dramatic arts, this offer didn't align with my future goals or what I wanted to build my life around. As Maz Jobrani would say, it wasn't a doctor or an engineer.

Plan A—getting into a top Iranian university to study either medicine or engineering—hadn't worked. But that didn't mean I couldn't become a doctor or an engineer. I'd just have to come up with an alternative plan. Plan

B was the next obvious step.

Sometimes, a dream is stepped on and misshapen. But that doesn't mean it is crushed. The more you care about a dream, the harder it is to destroy it, no matter what happens. While I wanted a college degree and wanted to become a doctor or an engineer, I knew it wasn't going to happen in Iran.

At first, of course, I was glum and despondent about not making it into one of my desired schools where I could work toward becoming a doctor or an engineer.

"Mehdi, feeling sorry for yourself will get you nowhere," I began to tell myself. "Quit sulking. Start figuring out how you're going to make this work." A lightbulb went off, illuminating my mind's eye. I was reminded of my favorite childhood book, *The Little Black Fish* by Samad Behrangi.

The book was published in 1967, when I was 16 years old. It is a small book, a long short story, really, of a little over 5,500 words. It's one of those tales that speaks to people of all ages—the type of story both a child and their parent can enjoy together.

Behrangi was 28 years old when his most famous book was published. A year later, he drowned amid widespread belief that the Shah's secret police had orchestrated the "accident." Beyond his writing, Behrangi was a teacher, a social activist, and a critic. He was renowned for his works promoting leftist ideologies, portraying poor urban children who, through their own efforts, rose above their bleak circumstances to live more fulfilling, richer, and freer lives.

The Little Black Fish reads like a fable with a hidden meaning beneath its poetic, dreamlike surface. The story is narrated by an old fish speaking to her 12,000 children and grandchildren, recounting the tale of a small black fish who wants to leave the safety of his known world, the small stream, to explore the world beyond. However, his mother and neighbors discourage him from doing so, poking fun at his curiosity. They question what's wrong with the world he is living in and insist their stream is good enough. The other fish warn him of the dangers of straying beyond the confines of the small stream.

But the little black fish ventures off on his own, disregarding their warnings. Along his journey, he meets various animals with different personalities – some friendly, others not. As he moves toward his goal of reaching the open sea, he is snatched up by a heron that flies into the sky. The little black fish tricks the heron and escapes back into the water, only to be swooped up again by the heron. He finds himself in the heron's gullet, where he meets another tiny fish. The little black fish comes up with a brilliant plan to save the tiny fish. The story ends with the grandmother saying that nothing was heard from the little black fish again.

The Little Black Fish, banned in prerevolutionary Iran, is a masterful allegory that depicts the struggle for liberation, offering encouragement and inspiration to the oppressed or those facing difficult circumstances to do what they must to break free, even if it means facing trials and dangers along the way. It is far better to have tried and failed than to never have tried at all. Regardless of the outcome, if you try, can that really be labeled a failure? The real failure is in not trying to better yourself or your situation.

When I first read the book at age 16, it spoke to me. I thought it was a wonderful story of being able to break free from your old environment and move toward a better life. But after getting rejected by the universities I wanted to get into in Iran, I revisited the book. This time, four years after my first read, it inspired me on a deeper level. I didn't just admire the little black fish for his courage and audacity in breaking free; I wanted to be the little black fish, moving toward a better life.

I decided to emulate that fish. I would leave my environment (my home country) and further my education in America. I would take the next steps toward my dream. That was, after all, the book's message: It's a big world out there. Don't limit yourself by staying in a place where you don't have the opportunities to live the life you want to live.

The more I thought about it, the more sense it made. America, after all, was known as the "home of the free and the brave." It had a respected system of higher education. It would open a whole new way of living for me, a whole new life.

I would be like that little black fish and cross the Atlantic Ocean to find what I couldn't in Iran.

Before I could rush off to the airport and grab a flight to America, I had one minor detail to address—the country's compulsory two years of military service. Without it, I couldn't apply for a domestic driver's license, much less a passport.

Sometimes, it seems, a dream takes a long time to unfold. But if the dream is worth it, then the time and energy spent on it is worth it too.

So, at age 19, I joined the Iranian Armed Forces.

I was assigned to train in the army's large artillery base in Kermanshah, specializing in tanks and all kinds of heavy equipment. Kermanshah, Iran's largest Kurdish-speaking city, is located in the western part of the country in the foothills of the Zagros Mountains, about 80 miles from the Iraq border. Winter temperatures can fall to 15 to 20 degrees below zero Fahrenheit. The snow can get quite heavy. In fact, when I arrived at the base in early December, the ground was covered in three feet of snow. The main road to the base was steep and unpaved, making it muddy and treacherous as the snow melted. More than 100 tanks were lined along the road, parked end to end. The massive base housed more than 50,000 military personnel.

After six months of combat training, I took an exam that determined that I would be stationed in northeastern Tehran's army garrison in Lavizān, a northeastern neighborhood in Tehran. I spent two years in the logistics department, managing transportation services like the military buses that moved personnel across the base each day.

Lavizān, nestled in the foothills of the Alborz Mountains, gets just as cold as Kermanshah and has just as much snow. Many wealthy people from throughout the Middle East flock to the region each year to ski in one of the many resorts.

Me at the military base in Kermanshah, Iran

But army life is hardly a vacation. I remember my army buddies and I took great care in waxing our dormitory floors each night, making them glisten and shine. If we didn't, our head sergeant would burst into the barracks at 2:00 a.m. and lead us out into the frigid weather—dressed only in our underwear—to do 250 push-ups. Just as your arms would inevitably begin to buckle (doing 250 push-ups at one time is nearly impossible), you'd feel the sergeant's boot grind into your back and push you into the slushy snow. I'm not sure which was sharper—his heavy heel grinding into my back, or the snow and ice that was freezing my whole body, particularly my hands.

"This isn't your mommy's house!" the sergeant would yell. "This is my house. And in my house, I have rules! Got that?" (Actually, his language was much more colorful than that. Sometimes, every other word was an f-bomb.)

"Yes, sir," I'd mumble, out of breath and with a mouthful of snow.

"I can't hear you!"

"Yes, sir!" I said, louder.

"Whose house is this?"

"Your house, sir!"

"Whose rules?"

"Your rules, sir!"

"Damn straight, Private!"

If you were lucky, he'd move on to berate the next guy. After about 30 minutes of torture, he'd tell us to "get our asses out of here and go inside." A string of derogatory names was thrown at us as we numbly lifted ourselves off the icy ground, teeth chattering and muscles aching. We'd stumble into the dorms, where we'd wrap up in our blankets and shiver for about half an hour before we could get ourselves to sleep.

My assigned group of eight men was responsible for serving three meals per day—breakfast, lunch, and dinner—to our squadron of 150 soldiers. We went to the kitchen in pairs, each man holding one end of the metal rod that supported our large pot of food. Outside of our daily responsibilities, we became good friends, joking around, playing cards, pulling pranks, and passing time with each other. I actually became very close with a Jewish boy in the group; we kept in touch for a while after being released.

To make some extra money—we earned about 70 tomans a month in the army—I picked up Friday shifts at Mr. Javadi's antique shop. I would also buy antiques here and there, selling them to other antique shops. By that time, of course, I had a pretty good understanding of the value of antiques, so this helped me earn a bit of extra cash.

Despite the occasional run-in with the head sergeant, my time in the army was relatively pleasant. To be honest, I enjoyed my time in the army. I was truly independent, meeting interesting people and making new friends. Above all, I was adapting to a new way of life, one that aligned with the discipline and work ethic I'd learned at the antique shop. As I matured and my day of discharge neared, I cast my eyes more and more on the new horizon that awaited me: the horizon that pointed toward America.

The times, as Bob Dylan had written a handful of years earlier, "they were a-changin'." My time in Iran was coming to an end. My grandmother, who acted as my surrogate mother after my birth mother passed, and whom I deeply loved, died while I was in the army. My oldest sister, Zari, was caring for her children while her husband worked as my dad's accountant and business manager. Dad's business was thriving; he'd hired several employees to help him. My oldest brother, Ali, was married and a father of two children. My younger brothers and sister were attending school. They, unlike myself, did not have to break up their education to help support the family.

"I want to go to America to continue my education," I said to my father a few months before my discharge. "Once I'm discharged, that's what I plan to do. In America, I'll get the education I want and need to be successful in life."

My father looked at me for a long moment.

"Mehdi," a small, bittersweet smile crossed his face, "I hate for you to be so far away, but I know it's the best thing for you. I trust your judgment."

I nodded, relieved. I was going to go regardless, but I wanted his blessing.

"I know I demanded a lot of you–more than I did of my other children– when I told you that you had to stop school and work full-time to help support the family. It was a great sacrifice on your part, and I wish I hadn't had to ask you that. But you did it. You helped us survive. For that, I am grateful."

"Thank you." We both had moist eyes.

"Now, it is your time, my son. It is your time to soar. All that you have gone through has made you much stronger and wiser than most young men your age. So, yes, when you are discharged, you go to America. You get the education you want. And you make us proud back here in Iran."

Chapter 5
Coming to America

On the evening of December 5, 1973, I stood in my father's kitchen, facing the man who had taught me so much about life and about being a survivor and fighter.

"Goodbye, *Haj Agha*," I said. "I will do my best to make you proud of me." I used this term because, in Islamic tradition, when a person completes the pilgrimage to Mecca (the birthplace of the Prophet Muhammad), they are often honored with the salutation "Haji." We would call our father "Haji Agha," combining "Haji" and "Agha," which translates to "mister." This gesture is used as a sign of respect.

"You already have. You have the courage to chase your dream. You are going to achieve great things, Mehdi."

With that, he gave me a quick hug. Before he turned away, I could see tears in his eyes.

My brother, Ali, and I walked out to his car, an old Paykan, the first Iranian-made model produced by Iran Khodro. He was now working as a pharmaceutical salesman for an Iranian division of Baxter International.

"Are you nervous?" he asked, glancing over at me. He was driving me to Mehrabad International Airport, which was then Tehran's primary international airport. I was unusually quiet.

I shook my head, then shrugged. "A little," I allowed. I'd never flown before. I had obviously never been to America or any foreign country. I knew less than 15 words in English. I didn't know the culture, the customs, or the expectations. So, yeah, I was a little anxious—but in a good way.

Nerves or not, I think, had my flight been canceled, I would have swum across the Mediterranean Sea and the Atlantic Ocean to get to America. I would have been like that little black fish, expanding its world however it could, no matter the risk.

Thankfully, however, my flight was not canceled.

My dream of continuing my education in America—my plan B—was about to become a reality.

The drive to the airport seemed to take forever. I kept glancing nervously at my watch, not wanting to be late and miss my flight. We took the Jenah Expressway, which passes directly by Tehran's Azadi Tower, a beautiful gateway landmark on the west side of the city. The tower, standing 148 feet tall and completely clad in brilliantly white cut marble, was built in 1971. When we passed it on the way to the airport, it was known as the Shahyad Tower (the Shah's Memorial Tower). Its name was changed to Azadi (Freedom) following the 1979 Iranian Revolution. Although it was not yet named Azadi, it certainly symbolized freedom for me.

Ali dropped me off and wished me luck. I watched his red taillights get smaller and smaller as he drove off. Before I carried my bags into the airport, I patted the secret compartment my stepmother had sewn into my boxers for my stash of US$150—the only money I had to my name. I was reassured by the little lump of money. It was probably safe to say I would be the only one on my flight with cash in his underwear. Call me a trendsetter.

Nervous as I was, I couldn't wait to board my first plane, cross the Atlantic, and begin a new way of life. If my flight had been canceled, I probably would have jumped in the water, swimming across the Mediterranean and Atlantic to take my first steps in America.

Like that little black fish, I was determined to expand my world, no matter the risk.

The airport was extremely busy, with waves of travelers jostling for position in ticket and baggage lines. I was used to being around crowds, but not to international travel. Muffled announcements were constantly being made over the loudspeaker.

I looked around for Hussein and became a bit frantic when I couldn't find him among the sea of travelers carrying or wheeling suitcases. Hussein and I had spent years bent over our textbooks as study buddies, dreaming of a life beyond night school. Now, as travelling buddies, our plans for a new life were becoming a reality. Or so I hoped.

I shuffled up to the front of the line and checked my bags. The agent was a bit heavyset, with a very calm and pleasant demeanor. This helped to calm my nerves. As I made my way to my gate, I found Hussein sitting and munching nonchalantly on an Anata F-15 chocolate bar.

"Hey!" he said, smiling, still chewing away. "You finally made it!"

"I did," I said, both relieved and a little irritated. We should have made more concrete plans about where to meet. My face and neck were sweaty, and my shirt was a bit damp against my skin. We sat together, waiting for our boarding call. Finally, I began to relax.

When we got on the plane, smiling Iran Air flight attendants greeted us, dressed in their sharp navy-blue uniforms. The polished buttons added a touch of sophistication. We found our seats and buckled in. I was lucky enough to get a window seat. The Boeing 747 jumbo jet had more than 500 seats, and it was nearly filled to capacity.

As the flight attendants began their required safety messages, I leaned my head against the headrest. The idea of crashing into the ocean with only a life preserver to help us was unnerving. Of course, the idea of crashing on land wasn't any more comforting.

My palms were sweaty as we taxied down the runway. Then, suddenly, the jet's engines screamed as the plane lifted off the ground. My stomach dropped as we ascended into the sky. Honestly, I was gripping my armrest so hard that my knuckles were white. Leaning toward the window, I watched my homeland slowly get smaller and smaller, the lights of Tehran twinkling before being snuffed out below the clouds.

After several minutes of climbing, the pilot leveled the plane, the seatbelt sign clicked off, and I relaxed my grip on the armrest.

"We're really doing this," I whispered to Hussein, a grin on my face.

"Apparently," he replied.

The flight from Tehran to Dulles International Airport in Virginia was about a 14-hour non-stop flight. (At the time, I assumed Dulles was in Washington, which caused a bit of confusion later.) Hussein struck up a conversation with Golnam, a young woman sitting next to him. She was also from Tehran.

"Why are you going to Washington?" she asked me.

I couldn't help but grin. "We're going to the U.S. as students on I-20s from Miami-Dade Community College." The I-20 is a document issued for international student status. It certifies that the international student has been accepted into a Student and Exchange Visitor Program -certified school in pursuit of an education.

"Oh! Very nice." She was quite beautiful. "What are you guys going to study?"

"Engineering," I said.

"Good for you. I wish you luck!"

When we asked her what she was doing, she told us she was meeting her fiancé in D.C.; he was a professor at George Washington University. They were getting married the following summer. She was a nonstop talker, very outgoing. She delighted in answering our questions about America, which she had visited three times before. Besides Washington, she and her fiancé had been to Baltimore, Philadelphia, New York, and Virginia Beach. She filled us in on each of the cities—the landmarks, museums, cuisines, her favorite restaurants, and the different types of people. It made for a much more pleasant flight than I'd expected.

After a meal, I dozed off for a while. I read a book for a bit and chatted with Golnam when I grew tired of reading.

"May I help you get a cab?" she asked after the flight attendants informed passengers that the aircraft was preparing for its descent. "It can be sort of crazy, especially because this is your first time in America."

"Thank you, we'd love the help!" I replied. It had been a long and emotional day. I was tired, and it would make the journey much easier if she were to help us.

"No problem," she said, smiling.

Unfortunately, it turned out to be a problem, although Golnam had the best of intentions. When we deboarded and waited together at baggage claim, Golnam got her bags first and then turned to see, apparently, her fiancé. At least I hoped it was her fiancé, because she ran shrieking into a man's arms, embracing him with a huge hug and a long kiss. Then, without a thought about her new Iranian friends that she had spent the day with and promised to help, she strolled off hand-in-hand with her fiancé. In a matter of moments, she was gone.

"So much for helping us," Hussein muttered.

"We'll figure it out," I assured him. "It can't be that hard."

Picture of me arriving at Dulles International Airport in Washington, D.C. on December 6, 1973

After getting our luggage, we found a payphone to call Mansour Adabi, Ali's childhood friend who now lived in Washington, D.C. Hopefully, he could suggest a place for us to stay. The payphone, however, was configured differently than the payphones in Tehran—which I rarely used anyway—and I was having trouble figuring out how to use it. It had three slots for coins and no directions. Was I supposed to put a coin in each slot? I rummaged for change in my pocket, but realized I only had bills—sewn, as I mentioned, into my underpants. (Perhaps the children's graphic novel series, *The Adventures of Captain Underpants*, created in the late 1990s, was modeled after me!)

I tried to dial without using money, hoping against hope that it would work. Of course, it didn't. I asked Hussein if he had any American coins, but he didn't.

"You need some help?"

I turned to see a large Black man in a gray custodial uniform behind me. He was holding a mop. The floor behind him was wet and had a yellow sign on it. I couldn't read the English words on the sign, but the image depicted a person falling.

I turned away quickly. I'm ashamed to admit that Hollywood had shaped my opinion of Black people, whom I had rarely met in Iran. In Hollywood, at least in the films I'd seen, they were portrayed as thieves, drug dealers, or gang members. This guy didn't look like any of those characters, but I was flustered and out of my element. Unfortunately, I fell back on the unwarranted bias that, ironically, I also became a victim of as I acclimated to my new country.

After a few moments of watching me struggle with the phone, he said, "You just need a dime. You got a dime? You put it in that slot there, then dial." He pointed to the dime slot.

"Dime?"

"Yeah, a coin. Like this." He fished in his pocket and pulled out a small, shiny coin. "Here. Just take this. You got the number you want to dial?"

I nodded, speechless and dumbfounded that this man was being so helpful to a couple of foreigners. Not at all the way Hollywood depicted Black people.

He slipped the coin in the slot. I heard the mechanical sound of it as it disappeared.

"Dial away," he mimicked punching the numbers on the phone. I couldn't understand what he was saying, so the gesturing was helpful.

I broke into a big smile, relieved. "Thank you, sir!" I said, using a few of the handful of English words that I knew.

As the man smiled and resumed his mopping, I dialed Mansour Adabi's number. If a person didn't answer the phone in Iran, it kept ringing—there was no answering machine to take a message. So, when I heard a female say something (I later realized she was saying, "We're sorry, this number is no longer in service"), I responded.

"Hello!" I said. "Is Mansour Adabi home? This is Mehdi, Ali Khosrow-Pour's brother."

But all I heard on the other end was a dial tone. Why would she hang up on me without answering my question? So far, I had met one very kind American and one very rude American.

Confused, I located a bathroom, went into a stall, and took a bill out from my secret compartment. Hussein and I walked into a gift shop to exchange my five-dollar bill for 50 dimes. It was my new favorite coin, my lifeline in America. I figured I could never have too many!

The lady behind the counter looked at me with curiosity. "You want – all dimes for this?" the clerk asked, holding up the bill I had given her.

Not completely understanding, but hearing the word dime, I eagerly shook my head. "Dimes," I repeated.

She handed me an entire roll of dimes from her register. I nodded and thanked her, and Hussein and I returned to the pay phone. I opened the pack of dimes, dumping all but one into my pocket. Their surprising weight gave me a sense of assurance.

I dialed Mansour's number again.

The same woman's voice answered and said what sounded like the same thing she'd said before, and the phone returned to a dial tone before I could even get a word in. I tried it two more times. With each call, I rushed to speak in hopes the woman answering would put Mansour on the phone. Of course, I got the same results—the same cryptic message, delivered in the same monotone voice before the phone went dead.

In 2004, Tom Hanks starred as an Eastern European man who was stuck in New York's John F. Kennedy Airport. The film, called The Terminal, was inspired by the true story of Mehran Karimi Nasseri, an Iranian who had lost his refugee passport and, ultimately, lived for 18 years in a terminal of Paris Charles de Gaulle Airport. I'm sure I had the same panicky feeling that Mr. Nasseri had when he learned he was unable to leave the airport because he had lost his refugee passport.

Fortunately, a kind lady noticed us wandering around the airport looking helpless and hopeless. She helped us book a bed and breakfast for US$15 a night (about US$90 today). The price was high, and it worried me, but the solution was better than being stuck in an airport.

After helping us secure the B and B, the lady turned to me. "Do you need help getting there?" she asked before noticing my quizzical look. "Transportation?"

I was still confused. (I am only guessing at these comments of hers, based on what transpired next.)

"Taxi? Car? Drive to bed and breakfast?" She mimicked holding a steering wheel.

A lightbulb went off for me. I smiled, relieved to understand.

"A car! Yes. Taxi?"

She was relieved too. And happy. She helped us flag a taxi and waved as Hussein and I got into the back seat. "Good luck!"

I smiled and waved at her, gave the driver the address, and breathed a sigh of relief. We were now, finally, going somewhere.

The driver gave us a friendly smile as he eyed us in his rearview mirror.

"Hey," he said, which I learned later was a common greeting. "How you guys doing?"

I gave him a quizzical look. He nodded, as if he understood.

"Are you new here? First time in America?"

I knew the words new and America. I nodded, smiling. "Yes! New in

America."

"Well, welcome to America!"

Again, I didn't exactly understand, but I could tell by his tone of voice and his facial expression that he was being friendly. As we drove, I took in the surrounding sites. "Washington very nice."

"We aren't in Washington yet," the driver said. "We're in Virginia."

"Virginia? Lost?"

He laughed. "No, not lost. Virginia is right next to D.C."

After about 30 minutes, we passed by a large cemetery (what I later learned was Arlington National Cemetery), crossed a river (the Potomac), drove by the Lincoln Memorial, and gazed in awe as we slowly cruised by the White House.

"The president's house," our driver pointed. I nodded, continuing to stare at the most important house in the country. Within minutes, we arrived at our B and B in the Dupont Circle neighborhood. We paid the driver, thanking him in broken English.

"Enjoy your stay!" he said as we closed the car door.

We waved. Then we turned and walked toward the home where we would spend our first night.

We were exhausted from the day's travel, the hubbub and commotion at the airport, the mix-up in reaching Mansour Abadi, and the difficulty in figuring out where to stay. I fell asleep within moments of my head hitting the pillow. I slept like a rock and woke refreshed and eager to explore.

At breakfast—pancakes and sausage links, vastly different from our usual morning meal—we discussed the previous day. We lamented about the long flight and laughed about our phone fiasco. We also talked at length about seeing the Lincoln Memorial and the White House on the way to our B and B. Most of all, we talked about the people we'd met, grateful for how kind everyone had been to us. They went out of their way to show patience and support. It made us feel at home.

At home.

In America.

Growing up as a poor boy in Iran, those are four words I never in my wildest dreams thought I would string together.

From our B and B, I finally connected with Mansour Abadi, my brother's friend. We met the next day at a coffee shop at Dupont Circle, seeking advice on the next steps on our exciting but uncertain journey. Our main plan, of course, centered around school. Although we had our I-20s from Miami-Dade Community College, we'd started looking at colleges closer to D.C. like Northern Virginia Community College, Prince George's Community College, and Montgomery Community College (the latter two in Maryland and all three within a half hour's drive of D.C.).

"Which college issued you your I-20?" Mansour asked as he sipped his coffee. Our booth was nestled in the rear of the mostly empty shop.

"Miami Dade Community College."

"Then there's no use in looking into these other colleges," he said. "You can get in big trouble with Immigration if you don't attend Miami Dade. Your student visa was issued based on the acceptance from that college."

"So, we can stop looking," Hussein said, eager to avoid the nasty D.C. winters.

"Yeah, go down to Miami, man," Mansour said. "The weather's warm all year, and the college girls sun themselves in these little bikinis." He raised a suggestive eyebrow and gave us a wink.

Yes, Miami didn't sound so bad. And we were already set up for school there. Both Mansour and Hussein were right.

After crashing on Mansour's couch and floor for nearly a month, Hussein and I bought two Greyhound tickets, boarded a bus, and headed south to sunny Florida.

The 21-hour bus trip took longer than our flight from Tehran to America.

It was packed with many different types of people—a figurative melting pot with Blacks, Whites, Latinos, Asians, and who knows who else. Our driver was a big, Black, cheerful fellow. Halfway through the trip, the air conditioner broke. And although the bus stank as we sweltered in the close heat, we didn't care. We were excited to be heading to Miami to start our journey in higher education!

Shortly before we arrived at the bus terminal in downtown Miami, I asked the driver if he knew where we could stay. He mentioned the name "YMCA." I wrote down the letters, clueless as to what they meant. Imagine my surprise when we walked out of the bus terminal and one of the first things I saw was a large sign with those four letters: YMCA. I was elated, relieved, and in dire need of a shower! "Come on, Hussein," I said, pointing at the sign. "That's the place the guy mentioned."

A sign posted at the front of the building read "Rooms for Let."

"What do you think that means?" I asked.

Hussein shrugged. "I don't know, but it says rooms. Maybe they have a place we can stay." As we approached the door, he held out his arm to halt my progress. "It says 'Christian.' We can't go in there."

"Why not?"

"Why do you think? We're not Christians!"

"So what? That doesn't mean we can't go in."

"What if they try to convert us? What if they don't let us stay unless we convert to Christianity?"

I shook my head in disgust. "Quit worrying. People have been so nice to us so far. They aren't going to bite our heads off. The least we can do is go in and find out if they have rooms for us, or if they know of some place we can go."

Hardly mollified, Hussein reluctantly followed me inside. Not surprisingly, the man at the desk was friendly. Realizing our command of the English language was moderate, at best, he took his time in explaining that they did have rooms that we could rent. And, no, nobody was going to try to convert us (I'd scowled at Hussein when he asked the man that question). We rented a single room with two beds and shared a communal shower area with other residents. This didn't bother me; I was used to communal showers from my time in the military. Poor Hussein took to washing himself at night with dishcloths in the bathroom sink.

"How can you let other men stare at you while you shower?" he asked me on our first night at the Y.

"No one's staring at anyone," I said. "We're just showering, that's all. It's a lot better than washing off in the sink."

"Not for me it isn't."

Our first task was to improve our English skills. Enquiring at the YMCA's front desk, I was steered to a nearby English language services center, where we enrolled in a month-long semi-intensive as a second English language (ESL) course for four hours each weekday. Students were required to speak English from day one. At the end of the month, our English was vastly improved.

We then enrolled in a second month-long intensive English course, which prepared us to communicate in all academic settings. This second course truly accelerated not only our understanding of the written language but also our ability to hear, comprehend, and use it. Yes, the courses were intense and far from easy, but they were critical for our academic success and our ability to assimilate into the culture. We now had a good basic understanding of the language and a foundation to build upon.

At a more practical level, we earned the certificate we needed to demonstrate our fundamental understanding of the language—a requirement for our student visa for us to pursue our education.

It's funny how things work out. When Hussein and I stood in the registration line for the ESL program, we spoke about moving out of the

YMCA. The Y was okay with me, but Hussein hated it. And, truth be told, I wouldn't have minded a nicer place to live. Neither of us, however, knew exactly where to look. Our lives were stressful enough without trying to find an affordable place to live in a nice neighborhood.

"Excuse me," the man behind us said. I turned around to see a White man, probably in his early 40s, standing with a Hispanic teenage boy.

"My name's Tony," the man said, extending his hand. I shook hands with him and introduced Hussein and myself.

"This is Eduardo. He's my friend's son, here to sign up for the program. Aren't you, Eduardo?"

"Sí," the boy said. He didn't look thrilled at the idea of learning a new language. "I mean, 'yes.'"

Tony laughed and clapped the boy lightly on the shoulder. He had an easy laugh and seemed to be a warm person.

"I couldn't help but hear you mentioning the YMCA," he said. "Are you guys looking for a new place to stay?"

"Yes," I said. "The YMCA is okay for a few days, but not long-term."

Tony agreed. "I've got a studio apartment that's open, and I'm looking for a good tenant. It's not huge, but it has two beds and it's in a nice neighborhood. Would you be interested in looking at it?"

"How much rent?" I asked. "What price?" My English was still in its toddler stage.

Tony paused. "I'm not looking to make a lot of money off it. I could rent it to you cheap—about 80 dollars a month. Would that work for you?"

Hussein and I looked at each other. Even though we didn't have jobs, we thought we could swing that rent. Surely, we could find work soon. We told Tony we'd love to see the apartment.

"Great! How about I come by the Y tomorrow at 4 p.m. to pick you up and show you the apartment?"

The next day, Tony picked us up and drove north on Biscayne Boulevard, the famed Gateway to Miami where members of the Rat Pack like Frank Sinatra, Sammy Davis, Jr., Humphrey Bogart, and Dean Martin used to congregate. The palm-lined boulevard was alive with colorful rhythms and beats of Cuban music throbbing from boom boxes balanced on young men's shoulders. There were artistic enclaves and sleek condominium towers in shades of coral and blue. We passed parks and country clubs that smelled of rich grilled meats. This was our first foray into North Miami, and we were playing the role of gawking tourists.

Tony eventually veered off Biscayne Boulevard into a nice neighborhood and to his home. The studio apartment, which was detached from his house, had two beds, a kitchenette, and a shower. The place was small, but it was clean. And the price was right. We eagerly accepted Tony's offer, signed a lease, and moved our few belongings from the Y to our new home the next day.

Once we moved in, we asked Tony if he could help us find jobs.

"You know who's always hiring?" he asked. "The restaurants on Biscayne Boulevard. I guarantee, you'll find work there."

The next day, we took the bus to our ESL class in North Miami—NE 125th Street and NE 2nd Avenue—about two miles from our apartment. I was excited to start classes and learn the language. I knew it would help me more fully assimilate into the culture. And, of course, I'd be better able to understand the instructors at Miami Dade.

After class, we took a bus back to Tony's neighborhood—now our neighborhood. We stopped to wander along Biscayne Boulevard, visiting restaurants to see if they were hiring. By our third rejection, I felt disheartened. It was a blow to my confidence. Hussein, tired and hungry, suggested we go home and try again tomorrow.

"Just one more place," I said. "Then we'll go home."

He shrugged and glumly agreed.

The next restaurant, a place called the Golden China, had cheap chairs, tables with peeling laminate, and a few faded Chinese lanterns hanging from the ceiling. But the enticing aroma of its food—the sharp ginger and tangy sauces—was wonderful. A thin old man with a long goatee stood behind the counter near the restaurant's entrance. He appeared to be checking receipts. He barely looked up as he pointed us toward the empty tables. "You can seat yourselves. A waiter will be with you in a moment."

"I'm looking for work," I said. "Are you hiring?"

The old man had already looked back down at his work. He looked up at me again. "You look for work? What kind work?"

"Any kind." But if I agreed to be his chef, we'd both be in trouble!

"Where you from?"

"Iran. We just moved to Miami a few days ago."

"You move from Iran?"

"Yes, we came here as students." I wondered why he cared.

"You bus dish? Put dish in bin, take to kitchen." He pointed to an employee who was carrying a bin full of dirty dishes, cups, and silverware back toward the kitchen.

"Oh! Yes! We bus dish."

"Okay." He reached his hand across the counter. I shook his hand, and Hussein followed suit. "I'm Mr. Lu. I your boss. I own this place." He pointed at me and asked, "You start tomorrow?"

"Yes, tomorrow's great."

"Good. This time tomorrow. We put you to work." Mr. Lu returned to working on his receipts.

Hussein and I stepped outside, and when far enough from the restaurant not to be heard, I let out a series of whoops, a testament to my overwhelming relief. I hadn't realized how tense I was about finding work! At least one of us found a job. We celebrated by going to McDonald's and indulging in Big Macs.

Over the summer, I continued bussing at Mr. Lu's restaurant. I enjoyed the fast-paced scene of Miami and was slowly adjusting to living in America. But I started to notice a difference between my acclimation and Hussein's, who maintained Iranian cultural habits and mannerisms as much as possible. He missed his homeland and kept as many ties to it as he could, including praying five times a day and patronizing Middle Eastern grocery stores. On several occasions, he'd even make a two-hour trip to buy just the right kind of lavash flatbread. While I missed my family, I was happy to be in America, following my dream of higher education and starting a new life in a new country—one with a seemingly endless array of opportunities.

I remember I was shocked the first time I saw a man wearing Bermuda shorts in public. In the Middle East, if a man showed his legs like that, he was considered gay. I quickly realized this was not the case in Miami, and (unless 90% of the men were gay) it was just a normal part of the American culture. Hussein, however, viewed these men with disdain, uncomfortable with seeing their hairy legs. I, on the other hand, went to a department store, bought a pair of Bermuda shorts, and proudly wore them around in public.

"What, are you gay now?" Hussein asked when he saw me in my shorts.

"I'm not gay, but I'm happy to be wearing shorts. And I'll bet my legs are a lot cooler than yours," I replied. He didn't appreciate my humor. I didn't care. When in Rome, right?

Customs obviously differ between countries. These same Miamians in Bermuda shorts might be shocked to see Iranian men, including my own father, wearing pajamas to the grocery store in Tehran. Just as Hussein assumed the men wearing shorts in Miami must be gay, Americans might assume that Iranian men wearing pajamas in public are homeless. No—they just want to be comfortable while shopping. Live and let live.

Hussein continued to go one way and I the other in adapting to our new home. Instead of lavash and other Middle Eastern foods, I gravitated toward cold beer and Big Macs. My refrigerator was stocked with cream cheese, baguettes, and pizza. I grew to love biscuits and gravy, French fries, chicken-fried steak, submarine sandwiches, hot dogs, and apple pie. Who doesn't love apple pie? I used to keep a McDonald's apple pie—the one wrapped in a pyramid-shaped box—in the glove compartment of my car at all times in case of an "apple pie emergency."

There were several reasons I was committed to adopting the customs of my new home. First, the array of choices in food and fashion was endless. And the freedom to choose was intoxicating. Like a kid in a candy store, I wanted to try everything. Second, I instinctively understood that limiting my cultural awareness and acceptance would be counterproductive to my cultural fluency and success, both financially and socially. I couldn't rise to the highest heights if I refused to become integrated with American culture. And embracing American customs was not a way of shunning my Iranian upbringing. Instead, it was a learning experience.

If I spoke only Farsi, spent all my free time with other Iranians or Middle Easterners, or focused solely on my old customs, I wouldn't get very far. Becoming somehow offended when someone offered me a beer or referred to the latest Rolling Stones song would only isolate me. I had already experienced a sense of exclusion in Tehran, where I'd been relentlessly ridiculed in school for my Gilak-accented Farsi, which I had gained in Northern Iran. I didn't want to go through that again.

I did notice, however—and this is common in most large cities in the United States—that there were enclaves of different nationalities. Miami has a large Cuban community. In New York, there are many Chinese and Italian communities. Many people within these communities choose to speak only their native language, shop exclusively in their own ethnic grocery stores, and essentially live the same as they would in their native countries. In doing so, they often ignore or cut themselves off from opportunities to broaden their horizons, enjoy the diversity around them, and live fuller and more successful lives.

I made a deliberate decision to choose a different path.

I had an amusing time trying to learn the American idioms I heard on the streets.

Bite the bullet. Go down in flames. Break a leg. Hit the hay. Americans sounded so violent!

Come rain or shine. Right as rain. The calm before the storm. They think a lot about the weather!

Ants in your pants. The elephant in the room. Get your ducks in a row. And they must be very fond of animals!

It became like a game for me, trying to pick up on the meanings of the strange sayings I was hearing.

I tried to explain the sayings to Hussein, but he was having none of it. "You and your stupid American sayings!" he snapped. "Who cares about chickens, anyway?"

In the summer of 1974, Hussein and I enrolled at Miami–Dade Community College, North Campus, in northern Miami. Miami Dade is not your typical community college. It is now the largest college in the Florida College System, with eight campuses and more than 100,000 students. Back then, though, there were just three campuses: North Campus, South Campus, and Downtown.

The night before the summer semester began, sleep eluded me as I stared at the ceiling. My mind swirled with countless questions: What if I can't make it? What if I don't understand the instructors? What if I can't keep up with my classmates? I'll be laughed out of school—and then what? If I fail, will I be a busboy forever or return to Iran with my tail between my legs?

I started sweating. Yes, it was easy to sweat in Miami, but this sweat came from fear. I was nearly paralyzed with anxiety. But I reminded myself that I'd climbed much bigger trees in my life so far, and there was no reason to be fearful. Rather, I should embrace the opportunity and forge ahead. With that, I finally fell asleep and woke up ready to start my first day of college.

Hussein and I rode a bus to the North Campus. As we walked onto campus, we gazed at the sparkling and pristine buildings. I entered my first class and grabbed a seat in the back. I was rather tall and did not want to block another student's view of the professor or the blackboard.

The first class ended with mixed results. Although I could understand the course content, I could only make out half of what the instructor said. I didn't have difficulty with the instructor's concepts; I just had problems understanding everything he was saying. Glancing around, I could sense that my peers were having no problem understanding the language. Their grasp of the English language was superior to mine.

Luckily, I wasn't completely lost, which was somewhat reassuring. While my ESL classes proved helpful, I found myself needing to study with both a textbook and a dictionary. I worked doubly hard to keep up due to my language deficiencies. Still, I formed friendships within the electrical engineering program with students from Iran whose language skills surpassed mine. These students, hailing from southern cities like Abadan, Ahvaz, and Bandar Abbas, helped me keep up with my lectures and classwork.

While the first few weeks of school were a bit rocky and anxiety-producing, I began to settle into a comfortable rhythm. My anxiety diminished, and I did well in my coursework. I bought a used red Schwinn 10-speed to commute the 15 miles between home, work, and school.

Purchasing the bike served as a reminder of my childhood aspirations in Iran. It also reminded me of the devastation of losing the bike that I so sorely wanted as a youngster—and the elation and freedom that came with the purchase of a bike three years later at age 15. I used that bike in the same manner as I was now using my 10-speed: to get to and from school and work. I was elated by the autonomy it afforded me as I zipped past stalled traffic, making my way between home, campus, and the Chinese restaurant. I probably rode well over 15 miles a day on that bike. It served me well.

I did quite well that first semester of school. My English skills noticeably improved, reflected in my strong grades. My fears about the language barrier proved unfounded. Each day, my command of the English language got stronger. To my surprise, however, I wasn't as passionate about the subject matter as I thought I would be. In fact, it bored me.

So, that fall, I switched to the business administration program, feeling a bit rebellious because Iranians are expected to excel in the STEM fields. Of the roughly 300 Iranians enrolled at Miami Dade Community College, about 299 were in one STEM field or another (mostly in engineering).

Again, I couldn't help but think of the little black fish navigating his lonely way toward an unknown ocean frontier. I, too, was no longer playing it safe by sticking with engineering. I was forging ahead, refusing to be held back by tradition, customs, or fear of the unknown. I was taking charge of my own destiny.

It was an important lesson: Be flexible with your dreams and goals. Thoughts and passions will change as you mature and experience life. Don't doggedly stick with what you thought you wanted when you were young. Remember to realize that your skills and interests may be better suited for another pursuit.

Forging ahead was a slow and arduous process. Still, my progress with the English language and the other challenges of adapting to my new country were fueled by my overwhelming desire to succeed—to make something of myself. I knew I was fortunate for this opportunity, with thousands of young Iranians back home who would give anything to trade places with me.

I continued learning the language, applying myself to my studies in preparation for a career in marketing, accounting, or finance. My new path created an unexpected bond with my father, who had been a businessman his entire life. He taught me the value of hard work. In fact, he modeled it for me my entire life—putting in long hours at the shop without complaint and never slacking off. I was becoming—as I'd heard people say—a "chip off the old block."

Outside of school, I immersed myself in American culture, eager to soak up every new experience. In 1974, I watched with fascination as Americans celebrated Hank Aaron becoming baseball's all-time home run king. It was a sport I knew little about, but it was extremely popular in the United States. Along with the rest of the country, I followed the Watergate scandal and President Richard Nixon's forced resignation. I reveled in the Rolling Stones singing "(I Can't Get No) Satisfaction." I loved The Who, especially "Won't Get Fooled Again." And I knew all the words to Aerosmith's song, "Same Old Song and Dance." On television, I watched *Sanford & Son* and *Happy Days*. I thought The Fonz, with his black leather jacket, embodied cool. I was also crazy about watching crime dramas like *Kojak* and *The Untouchables*. I got a taste of American humor by watching *All in the Family*, with its protagonist, Archie Bunker, always deriding his son-in-law, calling him "Meathead." I ate fast food, especially McDonald's, every day for lunch. On a daily basis, I'd devour an apple pie and a large order of French fries for lunch. *Blazing Saddles*, a movie about a railroad worker becoming the first Black sheriff in a small western town, spotlighted racism in America.

Unfortunately, I got a taste of racism up close and personal one evening as I was biking home from work. The day had already started off strangely enough, as I witnessed waiters at the Golden China scooping the remains of chow mien, fried rice, and white rice back into the communal pots being prepared for other diners.

"What are you doing?" I watched, stunned, as one of the waiters dumped another customer's leftover fried rice back into a big pot.

The guy shrugged and said, "Mr. Lu's wife told us to. It's just what we do here."

As I was riding my bike home that evening from the Golden China, a car skidded to a stop in front of me, forcing me to stop. A man, clearly intoxicated, leaned out the passenger window.

"Get off the road, you f*ing Mexican. Go back to where you came from!" He threw a plastic cup at me from his window, the sharp smell of alcohol smattering my shirt and splashing my face. The driver slammed on the gas, tires screeching as he fishtailed back into his lane and sped off, leaving me shaken and bewildered.

This was not my last exposure to racism in America. While most of the people I'd met so far had been kind and helpful, I began to realize that, like in many other countries, an undercurrent of racism flowed beneath the surface.

Comments like those from the drunk man didn't deter me. Instead, they just fueled my determination to succeed in this new country of mine, to show that I belonged. In 1975, I went on to earn my associate's degree in just one-and-a-half years rather than the customary two.

I was happy, but I didn't slow down to celebrate. I had, as another American colloquialism goes, "bigger fish to fry." So, after earning my degree, I immediately turned my attention to the next step in my journey: entrance into a four-year university so I could earn my bachelor's degree.

Chapter 6
My Academic Journey

Country singer Willie Nelson's number one hit "On the Road Again" wasn't released until 1980. But looking back, that could have been my theme song for the summer of 1975.

That was the summer I embarked on a cross-country road trip with my roommates, Ali and Jafar. We started in Florida, making stops in Huntsville, Alabama, through Tennessee to St. Louis, Missouri, to Las Vegas, San Diego, Los Angeles, and San Francisco. Then, we went back across the country to Hartford, Connecticut, and, finally, back down to West Palm Beach.

All told, we put more than 8,000 miles on four different cars. It makes me tried to even write that number now!

The main purpose of the trip was to scout out four-year universities that I was considering applying to in order to continue with my studies and earn my bachelor's degree. It also allowed me an opportunity to witness the vast diversity of American landscapes that I had been living in for almost two years. The depth and breadth of America—its mountains, plains, deserts, and fertile valleys; its bustling big cities and quaint small towns; its rivers, lakes, forests, and national parks must be seen to be truly appreciated. I had never been away from the East Coast and had indeed spent most of my time in Florida. Now, I was about to see large swaths of the rest of America—and there is no better way to see the country than to drive it, mile after mile, state after state, slipping from one highway to the next, all the interstates and roads and byways crisscrossing each other like a massive, intricate system of veins through which the country's lifeblood continuously pump.

The cherry on top was this: The trip, all 8,000-plus miles of it, cost next to nothing.

At the time, car transportation agencies existed for the sole purpose of shipping cars to owners. You could sign on for free to drive a car from point

A to point B, needing only to pay the cost of gas. I called such an agency in Miami, and they said they had a new Buick that needed to be delivered to St. Louis, Missouri. The agency gave us a week to drive it to St. Louis—ample time for us to stop off on the way in Huntsville, Alabama, where I visited Alabama A&M. We stayed overnight and did a campus visit the next day. Then, we drove north into Tennessee, staying overnight in Nashville before heading on to St. Louis the next day. While in Nashville, I called another car transportation company in St. Louis.

"We're dropping a car off in St. Louis tomorrow," I said. "Do you have a car that you need to be driven to California?"

The agent told me to hold on, and after a minute he said, "I do have a new BMW that needs to get out to San Francisco. Are you up for that?"

I conferred with Ali and Jafar. They eagerly nodded their heads. I shared their excitement, and thought it was a perfect way to see San Diego State University, another school I was interested in but figured I could never see in person because I couldn't afford the flight and there was no way I could drive my own Toyota Celica—a beater of a car—out there.

Grinning from ear to ear, I told the man that I was up for the job. I would drive a brand-new BMW to San Francisco, no problem.

"All right," he said. "We'll give you 10 days to get it out there. Can you do that?"

St. Louis to San Francisco is about 2,000 miles. We could do that easily—with plenty of time left over for a pit stop or two.

"Yes!" I said. "We'll be there tomorrow."

The next day, we drove into southern Illinois and over the Mississippi River, the second-longest river in the country. It spanned more than 2,300 miles from northern Minnesota to the Mississippi River Delta in the Gulf of Mexico. As we crossed into Missouri, we saw the Gateway Arc, the "Gateway to the West." This arch, the world's tallest monument at a height of 630 feet, was built to commemorate the westward expansion of the United

States. A surge of excitement washed over me. The stainless-steel structure gleamed, its graceful curve evoking a sense of adventure and possibility. I remember thinking, as we crossed the great river and took in the arch, that it was symbolically opening up a whole new world—the western United States—to us.

As Ali drove through the city, I carefully traced the winding highways along our paper map to locate the transportation agency (people nowadays can't survive without GPS and probably couldn't read a city map if you paid them). Soon, we pulled into the parking lot. As we headed toward the building's glass doors, we scanned the lot, looking for our BMW. Numerous cars of many colors, shapes, and sizes were on the lot. But I didn't see our next vehicle—or any BMWs!

Once inside, we met the man I had talked to the day before, and I filled out lengthy paperwork as the agent gave us our directions to deliver the Buick to its owner in suburban St. Louis. I was getting a little nervous because he hadn't mentioned the BMW that we were supposed to drive to San Francisco. Maybe he'd already contracted with someone else since I'd talked to him?

"And you still want us to drive the BMW to San Francisco, right?" I said, bracing myself for an unexpected change of plans.

"Absolutely," the agent replied. "It's around back. There've been some car thefts in the area, and we didn't want to risk it being stolen off our lot."

We happily followed the man to a warehouse behind the building and waited for him to drive the BMW out. As it emerged from the warehouse, its red coat of paint sparkled in the sun. It looked immaculate.

To top it off, the agent gave us a US$50 tip, which was not uncommon for car transportation agencies in those days. Gas at the time cost about 50 cents a gallon, meaning that the tip would cover the cost of gas for the entire trip to San Francisco.

"Now listen," the agent told us, "This is a new car. You have to make sure you get it to California in one piece. Can I trust you?"

"Of course," I said, trying to look as trustworthy as possible. "I'm a very safe driver. Never an accident."

"Good. And because it's a new car, you'll have to break in its engine gently. Meaning, don't go over 60 miles an hour. Okay?"

I nodded. "No worries," I said. "The car is in good hands."

Ali and Jafar drove the Buick to the owner's house in St. Charles, and I followed them in the BMW. The owner, happy to see his car, also tipped us. We were making out quite well financially on this trip! Knowing we had these extra funds let us focus more on our adventure and less on financial worries, making each stop along the way even more enjoyable.

"So, you're headed to California?" the man asked as we prepared to leave. I had told him of the next phase of our trip. "Have you ever been out there?"

"No, this is the farthest west we've ever been," I said. "In fact, until a few days ago, we haven't really been out of Florida."

"Well, you've got a lot of sights to enjoy along the way," the man smiled.

He was right. He was right. As we drove west on I-44, we were struck by the varying landscapes: the rolling hills and wooded areas of Missouri and the flat grasslands of Oklahoma. We continued on I-40 into the arid panhandle of Texas and the barren lands of eastern New Mexico, passing through the Chihuahuan Desert and the Rio Grande Valley into Arizona. We navigated the steep, winding roads of the San Francisco Mountains outside Flagstaff, Arizona. It truly is an amazing country, vast and diverse in both its terrains and its people.

For most of those miles, we'd been driving the BMW much faster than 60 miles an hour, despite the agent's warning. (In fact, we averaged nearly 75 miles an hour, covering about 1,600 miles from St. Louis to Las Vegas in around 21 hours.) We were, after all, three big kids on one of the longest joyrides in the history of mankind.

About the only time we had to slow down was in the mountainous areas near Flagstaff. Still, we made great time, and were several days ahead of our scheduled arrival in San Francisco. These several days, we thought, should be spent in Las Vegas. "Sin City" was situated in the Mojave Desert and was world-renowned for its entertainment industry and casinos.

We pulled up to the Tropicana casino hotel, where a valet, seeing our shiny new BMW, hustled over to park our car for us. He probably assumed we were rich kids coming to blow our (or our parents') money on blackjack, poker, craps, and the jackpot machines. In reality, we were three poor guys who wanted to experience the thrill of a Vegas casino for the first time and try our hand at the jackpot machines without going bankrupt.

Las Vegas Boulevard, or "The Strip," has iconic hotels and attractions. There were pedestrian bridges crossing the major road and tons of entertainment to beckon tourists. For less than US$35, we booked one night at the Tropicana, with two king-sized beds, a pullout couch, plush chairs, stylish coffee tables, a sparkling bathroom, tasteful art on the walls, and a beautiful view of the city spread out before us. Our breakfasts were free—they wanted you to spend all your money gambling, and we obliged. The brightly lit jackpot machines' spinning reels, as well as their symphony of bells and jingles, added to the thrill of each pull. There was so much to see and do inside our hotel that we barely ventured outside. We enjoyed our visit—staying in the beautiful hotel for next to nothing, getting free food, and enjoying the view from our room on the 20th floor, especially at night when the city was all lit up.

From Vegas, we drove another 340 miles to San Diego—a quick trip for us compared to what we had gone through a few days before. San Diego State, a university with a top-ranked business program, was one of the schools I had targeted. In a way, it mirrored Miami. I'd just be switching the Atlantic Ocean for the Pacific. It wasn't hard to fall in love with San Diego State's campus. There were palm trees everywhere, pristine sidewalks, and southwest-style buildings. I was very impressed and thought it could be a good place to get my bachelor's degree, though it was so far from my newfound home in Miami. So, I tucked away the possibility of attending the university, adding it to my list of options.

After a two-night stay with a friend in Los Angeles, we undertook the last leg of the journey to deliver the BMW. We arrived in San Francisco on a gorgeous summer day, bringing the BMW to its new owner's mansion on top of a massive hill that overlooked a breathtaking view of the Golden Gate Bridge and the bay beyond.

"You guys drove all the way from St. Louis?" the man asked, shielding his eyes from the sun as he spoke.

"Yes," I said. "It was a long drive, but very beautiful."

He nodded. "It is. Where are you guys from? You live in St. Louis?"

"No, we're from Florida," I said.

"Whoa. That's a long way from home."

"It is," I acknowledged. "But not as long as from Iran."

"That's where you're originally from?"

"Yes, sir. I came to America to study. I'm picking out my college to get my bachelor's degree."

He eyed me appreciatively. "Good for you. Here, this is for getting my car home in one piece. It's good to see someone making something of themselves."

I thanked him, and then it was my turn to be shocked when he handed me a US$200 tip. "That's for your college fund. Every little bit helps, right?"

We shook hands. "That's very kind. Thank you."

I had called another car transportation agency in San Francisco shortly before we arrived in the city. They had a Chevy that needed to go to Hartford, Connecticut. We had 10 days to drive 3,000 miles—a piece of cake for us. We were beginning to feel like Formula 1 drivers. Then, we'd take another car back to West Palm Beach.

It was amazing how we just leapfrogged all over the country, taking one car from Miami to St. Louis, a second car from St. Louis to San Francisco, a third vehicle from San Francisco to Hartford, and a fourth from Hartford to West Palm Beach. Thus, we completed our road trip of 8,044 miles.

Along the way, I drove through forests, deserts, mountains, and plains. I saw national parks and historic landmarks. And I passed through Georgia, Alabama, Tennessee, Illinois, Missouri, Oklahoma, Texas, New Mexico, Arizona, Nevada, and California on the way out. On the way back, we traveled through Nevada, Utah, Wyoming, Nebraska, Iowa, Illinois, Indiana, Ohio, Pennsylvania, New York, Connecticut, Maryland, Virginia, North Carolina, South Carolina, and Georgia—before landing back home in Florida. That's 26 states—more than half the country! If I were a school kid reporting on his summer vacation, I would have had quite a story to tell!

Exploring the United States to find the right college was a liberating experience. Each journey to a different city and campus brought new perspectives and possibilities, allowing me to envision my future in various ways. It was a luxury to have the freedom and access to resources to travel. The trip was not just about finding a place to study, but about discovering where I felt a sense of belonging and where I could see myself growing academically and personally.

Upon returning from my exciting trip across the country, however, I had a decision to make about what institutions or universities I would choose to continue my education and earn a four-year college degree.

After Hussein moved on to Houston, where he had been accepted to Texas Southern University, I began sharing a two-bedroom apartment on 25th Street and NW 2nd Avenue with two other college students. I also started a new job—another big plus. I traded dirty dishes and clearing tables for a position as a valet parking attendant at Fontainebleau Miami Beach. The high-end resort catered to the jet-set crowd, a mix of wealthy travelers, celebrities, and powerful professionals. I was paid a measly US$1.25 per hour as a valet, but I more than made up for it in tips (sometimes, I'd get a

US$3 tip—equaling about $17 today—not a bad tip for driving a guy's car up to him and handing him the keys). I'd smile, be gracious and friendly, and hold the door open for the driver's wife. My friendliness and service paid off. On an average day, I'd make US$15 in tips. But on my peak days, I'd finish my shift with more than US$100 of tips in my pocket.

The work presented a unique set of challenges and rewards. I polished my organizational skills and developed an ability to remain composed under pressure. Plus, interacting with guests from all walks of life provided me with opportunities to network and build relationships.

My experience only reinforced what I'd learned from my father: Work is work. Keep your nose to the grindstone and give whatever you're doing all that you have. If you do, you'll do things most people couldn't even imagine. If you want something bad enough, and you work hard enough, you can attain the loftiest of goals.

Like attending the second-most expensive private university in the nation and graduating early.

I'd already been accepted to several universities, including Alabama A&M, San Diego State, and the University of Miami. The allure of the University of Miami in Florida, however, was strong. Florida had come to feel like home—San Diego seemed (and was) so far away. So, Miami had a home-court advantage in my decision-making process.

In addition, neither Alabama nor San Diego would accept all the credit hours I'd earned at Miami Dade. The University of Miami, with its relationship to the nearby community colleges, would accept my hours and allow me to take up to 18 credits per semester for a fixed rate. Plus, it provided housing. At Miami, I could maximize the value of my education, piling up my credit hours quickly and graduating ahead of schedule.

Unfortunately, Miami was the country's second-most expensive private school after Harvard. This meant that I would need to continue my demanding work schedule while completing my degree.

I made my decision and enrolled at the University of Miami in the fall of 1975.

I won't kid you—my 18 months (I graduated early, as I had planned) at the University of Miami weren't easy. I would often scrimp on food. I made do with all types of cheap meals, from a large order of fries, microwaved noodle soup, or spaghetti with marinara and cheap bread. On the nights I worked at the Fontainebleau, I was, at least, given a complimentary meal. Believe me, I took advantage of it! I looked forward to their food my whole shift. Their food's quality and cooking were "a little better" than mine!

Me graduating from the University of Miami in August 1977 with degree (BBA)

I'd get tired, but I didn't complain. I was like a racehorse with blinders on. I was intensely focused. I didn't allow myself to get distracted; I just kept looking straight ahead, reminding myself why I had come to America in the first place.

I tuned out distractions, attended every class, and carefully managed my money. First and foremost, I had come to continue my education. That was my all-consuming goal, and nothing was going to keep me from it.

I never missed a class in those semesters at Miami. A lot of my classmates skipped class and partied not just on the weekends but throughout the week. Many of my peers were supported by their rich parents, blowing through their money. They just didn't care. They didn't have to pay for their tuition, rent, or meals.

I, however, was responsible for supporting myself, paying for every penny of my education and my life. To me, missing class, no matter how tired I felt, would be like ordering a lobster dinner at a fancy restaurant and not taking a single bite. You're paying for it—why not take full advantage of what you're paying for?

I kept my eyes on the prize: a bachelor's degree in business administration.

Most of my classes were engaging, especially marketing and accounting. To satisfy my general education requirements, I also took courses in literature and history—and loved them. And to think, only two years earlier, I could barely speak English! (Granted, I was reading copies that had Farsi translations in the margins of the pages.) Now, I was enrolled in—and excelling in—a literature class!

One day after world literature, my professor, Peter Johnson, took me aside.

"Mehdi, out of all my students, you're the one who is most involved," he said. "You're always asking questions and participating in our dialogue or commenting on a passage. Don't take this the wrong way, but I never would have thought that a student from Iran would be my most animated student in class! What are you majoring in?"

I smiled. "Accounting."

"Would you ever consider changing your major to literature? You really seem to have taken to it."

"Well, I haven't really thought about it," I said.

"Give it some thought," Professor Johnson said.

I nodded, thanking him as I left his classroom. I knew there was no way I was going to switch to literature. What would I do with a literature degree? With a business degree, I could find good work in sales and move up the ladder into management and operations. It was a very valuable degree. But literature? No way. Like the little black fish, I had already exited the pond. First, I'd come to America. Second, I was eschewing engineering and medicine for business. I wasn't going to go off the deep end by majoring in literature!

As I delved into my core business courses, my marketing, advertisement, and management classes aligned with my own experiences, from working in the antique shop back in Tehran to watching my dad run his business. For example, my dad paid close attention to his long-term customers, offering them the highest quality services and discounts. Through my marketing education, I understood how his behavior applied to customer retention concepts. It's much easier to keep your current customers happy—even if you have to part with some of your financial margins—than to find new customers altogether.

Accessing an intuitive body of knowledge and studying the same concept in a formal educational setting was validating. It was like learning to drive a car on your own before taking a formal driver's education class to study the rules of the road or to parallel park. Later, when I became an entrepreneur, I would benefit greatly from this double education.

When you go into business, you can't rely solely on academic preparation. But street smarts alone, without any formal training, won't give you entry to many fields either. Connecting commonsense, practical knowledge with a rigorous education helped me gain an advantage in business.

In the 1970s, the University of Miami was known as "Suntan U." It offered the perfect combination of warm weather, beautiful beaches, attractive students, and a legal drinking age of 18—it's not hard to see why it was known as a party school. It was a place where the rich kids could register for class, major in fun, and (hopefully) walk away with a degree in four or five years.

It was an ideal university for my good friend, Steve, and many of our other classmates. As I said, that was not my approach to school.

In a campus parking lot filled with Mercedes, Ferraris, and Lamborghinis,

Steve fit right in with his Mercedes-Benz 450SEL convertible.

For extra money, I was tutoring students in computer programming and a statistical software suite. Basically, I programmed for these students in exchange for cash. One afternoon, after tutoring a student from New Jersey, I saw Steve get out of his car near the student center's front gate. His vehicle, which was nearly parked on the lawn, had a parking ticket nestled under its windshield wiper. From that day forward, I'd always spot Steve's convertible parked in the same location—and always with a parking ticket. Eventually, I asked Steve about these parking violations. Why would he pay hefty fines to park illegally?

"I drive this car for the chicks," Steve said bluntly. "I'm not going to get anything out of it by parking it in the back of the lot." Obviously, Daddy was footing the bill.

I chuckled when comparing Steve's circumstances to my own. I barely scraped together enough money to buy a 1963 Plymouth Valiant, a car I parked at the farthest end of the lot so nobody could see it. After a minor accident, I could no longer open the driver's side door, and I had to get in and out through the passenger side. My car was barely street legal, while my friend accumulated endless US$10 citations to impress would-be sweethearts.

My Iranian roommate, Jeff, also had a wealthy family who supported his personal and academic lives. Like me, Jeff would register for 18 credit hours each semester. By the end of each semester, however, he had usually completed about half of those hours. On weekends, Jeff's Cuban girlfriend would come over. They would lock themselves in his bedroom, have sex, and smoke marijuana for days. With an en suite bathroom, they had no need to emerge from their benders. But it left him little time for his studies.

My routine was the opposite. I spent most of my time in the library, working around the clock as a tutor or a valet. When the client traffic was light, I'd find a vacant car at the hotel and crack open a textbook.

In the summer of 1977, I graduated with a bachelor's degree in business, majoring in accounting. In less than four years, I had earned an associate's degree in art from Miami–Dade Community College and a bachelor's degree in business administration from the University of Miami, leaving people like Jeff in my wake.

As I prepared to cross the stage to accept my diploma, memories flooded back to my pivotal decision to enroll in night school when I was 14 years old. I was forced to make that decision because I had to work to help support my family. That's a big burden on a 14-year-old's shoulders. It's one that the average 14-year-old American couldn't even fathom. But I always admired my father's tireless work ethic and dedication to providing for our family. I witnessed his struggles to make ends meet, and I felt a strong sense of responsibility to alleviate his burden. He worked very hard, but times were tough, and he had no education to help him rise above his situation.

Okay, I told myself. I will help. I love my father and my family.

But I will not give up my dream of a better life.

And that dream, that better life, hinged on education. My 14-year-old mind knew that.

So, I worked. I attended night school. I kept my eyes on the prize.

And when the time was right, I came to America to advance my education. Its education system was top notch. I knew this country was the place that would propel me forward. I was not deterred by my challenges with the English language or my lack of funding. I didn't need connections because I had self-determination and self-motivation. I had willpower and perseverance. I, alone, would determine my future. And I alone would determine my destiny.

All of that flashed through my mind as I walked across the stage in my cap and gown, wishing Dad could be there to witness my journey. And I felt surprisingly calm as I shook the provost's and then the university president's hands.

I knew my father was proud of me. Every parent wants their child to accomplish more than they did—to live a better life than them. I was happy, but I knew that I was far from finished.

After crossing that stage, another thought flashed in my mind.

In my life's marathon, I'd just passed the halfway mark. It's a point where many people falter and give up. I, however, found myself rejuvenated, gaining a second wind to go many more miles in my education. Like a runner finding their stride, I pressed on, driven by the knowledge that my determination would take me to the finish line. Lots of people can't even make it to the 13.1-mile mark!

The next leg of my race covered 174 miles—the distance from Miami to Melbourne, the location of the Florida Institute of Technology (FIT and later Florida Tech). I visited my friend, Ali Ansari, at the school after my graduation in 1977. I was impressed with the campus. Melbourne was a relaxed college town, with a quiet pace of life. The FIT campus was on Florida's eastern coast. It was also called the Space Coast due to the nearby Kennedy Space Center and Cape Canaveral. In fact, all orbital launches from American soil from 1961 through 2011 that carried NASA astronauts departed from either the Kennedy Space Center or Cape Canaveral.

I spent two days on campus visiting an admissions officer on my second day. I told her that I was interested in applying to their Master of Business Administration (MBA) program.

"Wonderful! Where did you earn your undergrad?" she asked.

"Well, I recently graduated from the University of Miami with a bachelor's in business administration."

Outside her window, I could see students walking across a bright green lawn. Palm trees, their fronds moved by a brisk breeze, were waving in the air. A few students were throwing frisbee back and forth.

"We have many students come up from Miami," the admissions officer said. "If you were to attend here, you'd get an experience that few other MBA programs can offer. You'd be rubbing elbows with corporate professionals from Cape Canaveral and Harris Corporation. So, you'd be learning and working with some highly successful businesspeople who, like you, want to further their education and their careers."

I knew of Harris Corporation's strong reputation as a federal contractor. They produced wireless equipment, tactical radios, electronic systems, night vision equipment, and various surveillance solutions and weaponry. Although the company is no longer operating, having disbanded in 2019, they were a major force at the time.

I was more than intrigued. I told the officer that I'd forward her my Miami transcript as soon as it was official and send her my graduate school entrance exam, and graduate management admission test. These were required when applying for admission to a graduate management program, such as an MBA program.

There was an abundance of tests, tests, and more tests! There were lots of hoops to jump through. But it would all be worth it!

I was admitted to FIT for the fall semester of 1977.

Was I motivated? Well, I ramped up my studying, falling one B+ short of a 4.0. I completed the MBA program, which is set up for students to finish in two years, in 11 months. I did nothing but eat, sleep, and drink my MBA program.

And work. Of course, I still had to support myself and pay for tuition, rent, and necessities like food. Yes, McDonald's fries were still a staple of my diet. The fries were cheap and relatively filling thanks to all the oil they were fried in.

To keep the fries coming and tuition paid, I worked three jobs: a cab driver, a daytime waiter, and an evening maître d' at a nearby country club's restaurant. I got to keep half of my fares as a driver. Most of my cab business centered around Melbourne's regional airport, with a steady stream of customers from Cape Canaveral or the military base by Cocoa Beach.

I never wasted a minute while I was on my rounds. At the airport, while awaiting a flight's arrival, I'd take out my textbook, grab a highlighter, and study until my next passenger came.

By the end of each night, I flopped onto my bed, quickly falling into a deep sleep. A bed had never felt so good! I had a roommate, but we barely spoke—not because we didn't like each other, but because we barely saw each other. When I think back on my brief time in Melbourne, I picture myself lugging a heavy backpack all across campus, from the library to my classrooms to the student union and back to my apartment. By the end of the day, my shoulders ached because I would take all the books that I needed for the entire day. I felt a bit like a pack mule.

Although I focused on my coursework, I came up just shy of a perfect 4.0. Regardless of my strong grades, I was bored by the subject matter and felt it duplicated my undergraduate courses. At that time, business schools centered around multinational corporations, which proved to be not all that helpful because about two-thirds of all businesses in the United States were small- to medium-sized organizations. Thus, knowledge of how global corporations operated wasn't practical for the majority of MBA students because they were going to work for much smaller operations. I recognized that fault even back then, and I experienced it from a different vantage point when, years later, I was running my own business. Over the years, I've hired dozens of MBA graduates who were ill-prepared to work for smaller companies.

As the admissions officer had told me, there was a big bonus to enrolling in the school's MBA program: I took courses with and learned from experienced corporate professionals from Cape Canaveral, Harris Corporation, and other companies in the Space Coast region. In many ways, I learned more from my cohorts than I did from some of my professors.

I'll never forget one afternoon in an organizational behavior class. The professor was talking about employee motivation and pontificating about salaries and benefits. When a few students argued that money was just one important way to motivate employees, the professor smirked.

"Oh, really? So, we could do away with salaries and employees would approve?"

The student sitting next to me, Mike, was observing the conversation with a frustrated look on his face. Mike had proven to be a very sharp student with keen insights on several issues. Now, he raised his hand.

"Mike, do you have something to add?" the professor asked, still smirking. I could tell he wanted to prove he was smarter than all his students.

"Yeah, I was just going to say that I did a study on employee motivation. And I know that while wages are important, they're pretty far down the list of motivational factors for employees," Mike said.

"Is that so?" the professor said. His smirk wavered. "Why don't you tell us what you learned."

"Actually," Mike said, sitting up at his desk and looking around first at his classmates and then at the professor, "the top factors in employee motivation are appreciation and recognition for a job well done. Most employees, especially in large corporations, feel like they're not seen or heard—like they're just little cogs in a big machine. So, it means a lot when their bosses recognize their contributions, their work, and their value to the company."

The professor tersely nodded. "Yes, appreciation is good. But I still think—"

"Coming in a close second is being in the know about company matters," Mike continued. "You need buy-in from your employees or, no matter how great your plan is, it's going to be hard to execute. It's the idea of being part of something greater than yourself. If they buy into your vision, amazing things can happen."

Mike went on to list several other factors that were critical to employee motivation: an understanding attitude from management, job security, interesting work, loyalty from management, good working conditions, and career advancement opportunities.

"So," the professor said once Mike was finished, "you've written a paper on this. You've researched it. That's good, very commendable. But sometimes there's a disconnect between the theoretical and the practical. Once you're out in the real world, you might find that it really does boil down primarily to wages."

"With all due respect, Professor Hughes, I've been working for Harris for several years now. I've been part of a program that's put a lot of what I just talked about into practice. And employee motivation and loyalty have skyrocketed."

That was a huge learning moment for me, illustrating the value of questioning authority—something you'd never do in Iran. Mike wasn't being confrontational or offensive with Professor Hughes. He respectfully stated his case and presented facts to back it up. While I learned that theory and research are valuable, they don't trump practice. Learning from books is valuable, so long as it prepares you for, as Professor Hughes would say, the "real world."

I look back with amazement on the 11 months I spent in Melbourne. Where did I find the stamina and the drive to carry the maximum load of classes? How did I avoid collapsing halfway through my studies? I'll never know. It was grueling. It was intense. And it was mind-numbing.

But it was worth it. My goal at FIT was to get in and out as fast as possible. No other student who I entered the program with earned their degree as quickly. But I wasn't competing with my peers… I was competing with myself. And I won!

Chapter 7
Interruption in My Education Because of a Revolution

Nova Southeastern University—then known as Nova University—was a private institution of higher education in Fort Lauderdale, Florida and about a half-hour from my apartment. Its history traces back to the 1964 founding of Nova University of Advanced Technology. Nova merged with Southeastern University of the Health Sciences in 1994 to form the present Nova Southeastern University. I was impressed with the faculty there and with their Doctor of Business Administration (DBA) program. In 1920, the Harvard Graduate School of Business Administration, now Harvard Business School, introduced its DBA program. This new applied graduate degree program aimed to produce scholars who could apply business theory into practice in corporate settings. The University of Chicago's School of Business introduced its DBA program shortly after Harvard, followed by the University of Pennsylvania's Wharton School of Business. This type of degree equips students with advanced leadership skills, opens doors to higher-paying positions in management, and provides various research opportunities.

So, in September of 1978, I applied to Nova University Graduate School of Business Administration, and I was admitted to start the final leg of my academic journey to obtain my doctoral degree.

The DBA program offered at Nova University was very similar to executive MBA programs offered at many graduate schools of business. All classes were offered on Saturday and Sunday so professionals could attend. Classes were taught either by faculty of Nova University's Graduate School of Business or by well-known professors from top-notch research institutions like Harvard, the University of Georgia, or Princeton University. These professors would be flown to the South Florida campus to enjoy the nice warm weather while getting paid to teach a class! It was a good breakaway for many of them.

During the first year of my doctoral studies, things were heating up in a major way back in my home country. A little background for you: The

Pahlavi dynasty ruled in Iran from 1925 to 1979. Mohammad Reza Pahlavi was the last shah (king) of the Imperial State of Iran, ruling from 1941 until he was overthrown in the Iranian Revolution of 1979. This revolution saw the government of Iran change from a monarchy to a theocracy, the latter ruled by Ayatollah Ruhollah Khomeini, a religious cleric who headed one of the rebel factions that overthrew the Shah. Khomeini had been exiled to Iraq and later to France by the Shah from 1964 to 1979 before he returned to Iran once the Shah's government was overthrown.

In August 1978, just as I was beginning my doctoral program, four men doused the Cinema Rex in Abadan, Iran, with airplane fuel and set it ablaze. The fire killed upwards of 577 people and was directly linked to the Shah's government and intelligence services. This fire not only killed hundreds; it showed Iranians the lengths the Shah's government would go to maintain power.

The ruling Pahlavi dynasty blamed Islamic militants for the fire; the anti-Pahlavi protesters blamed SAVAK, the notorious Iranian secret police. According to Roy P. Mottahedeh (1985, p. 286), author of *The Mantle of the Prophet*, "thousands of Iranians who had felt neutral and had until now thought that the struggle was only between the Shah and supporters of religiously conservative mullahs felt that the government might put their own lives on the block to save itself. Suddenly, for hundreds of thousands, the movement was their own business."

While protests had been taking place throughout 1978, the fire catalyzed large-scale strikes and demonstrations throughout the remainder of the year. In November, student protesters took over the University of Tehran. The city erupted into a full-scale riot after a fight on the university's campus between the demonstrators and the police turned deadly. Government and police buildings were seized and burned. The British Embassy was partially burned and vandalized, and the American Embassy nearly suffered the same fate.

The Shah, waffling in his decisions and further weakening his power, gave conflicting orders to the army and police, finally instructing them not to initiate full violence in his last desperate attempt to stay in control of the country. The Shah appointed a military government and, on November 6, made a televised speech in which he said he heard the voice of the revolution but could not support it. He would, however, work with the opposition to bring democracy to Iran and form a coalition government.

The speech backfired. The revolutionaries sensed the Shah's weakness. Ayatollah Khomeini, for his part, took a harder stance: He said there would be no reconciliation with the Shah and no "coalition government." He called on all Iranians to overthrow the Shah through his fatwa, a ruling by a recognized authority, in this case Ayatollah Khomeini, to act based on Islamic laws.

From December 10 through 11, between six and nine million anti-Shah demonstrators marched across Iran—more than 10% of the country's population. For comparison's sake, the famous French and Russian revolutions involved just 1% of their populations.

In January 1979, Shah Mohammad Reza Pahlavi fled the country. Great joy and spontaneous celebrations spread throughout the land. Millions poured onto the streets, and virtually every remaining sign of the monarchy was torn down.

One month later, Ayatollah Khomeini returned to Iran to become the supreme religious leader of the new revolutionary government. Within 10 days of his return, the monarchy fell, and Ayatollah Khomeini oversaw the Iranian government. In a referendum that March, 98% of Iranian voters approved the country's shift to an Islamic republic. In December 1979, Ayatollah Khomeini became the Supreme Leader of Iran.

All was far from well. Some say that from 1979 to 1982, Iran was in a revolutionary crisis. Its economy had collapsed, and the military and security forces were in disarray. The Western world was in denial, unwilling to accept the fact that the Pahlavi dynasty had ended and the Iranian Revolution was in full control of the country.

By December 1978, I had been in the United States for five years, focusing on pursuing my educational goals. By that winter, it had, however, become increasingly difficult to maintain that focus on my education, given all that was taking place back in Iran. I devoured the newspapers and newscasts to learn the latest, and occasionally spoke on the phone with my brother Ali and my father for updates.

The Shah had oppressed the people of Iran. SAVAK tortured and executed many of those in opposition to his regime. Sometimes, SAVAK forces would find those in opposition, bind their hands, tie cinder blocks to their legs, and drop them in a lake from a helicopter.

Even my own father was not immune to SAVAK brutality. Dad, during the pre-Shah period, had belonged to the national party of Iran led by the former prime minister, Dr. Mosaddeq, whose government was overthrown by the Shah's U.S.-funded coup of 1953. Almost two-thirds of Iranians at the time were members of the National Party, including my father. Now, years later, they were being questioned by SAVAK.

One day, several SAVAK agents showed up at my father's place of business, blindfolded him, and took him away. For two days, our family did not know his location. We feared for his safety, looking everywhere and contacting the authorities. Finally, after 48 hours, the SAVAK agents dropped my father at an undisclosed location, forcing Dad to find his way home. For two days, they had interrogated him about his involvement with the National Party and his relationships with its leadership. He repeatedly told them he was just a regular dues-paying member.

Throughout the uprisings, many believed the military would crack down on the rebels and put an end to the chaos. However, the military, under the government of the Shah, became more and more reluctant to attack demonstrators. Many soldiers, in fact, defected to join the demonstrators.

This was the beginning of the end for the Shah and his regime. Soon, there was jubilation in the streets throughout the country as his regime was toppled. That celebration extended far beyond the country's boundaries to Iranians living all over the world, including one particular student working on his doctoral degree in Florida.

As I was reading and watching the news about the revolution, I became increasingly restless. When the Shah fled the country in January 1979, I was elated. The longstanding Pahlavi dynasty, which had begun in 1925, was coming to an end. I had never harbored such hope in my heart for my home country as I did then. However, another post-revolution desertion became apparent—a "brain drain" as some of the brightest minds with university degrees and real-world expertise left Iran for more stable countries.

As the weeks passed and events unfolded, work on my doctoral degree, as important as education always was to me, began to dim as my attention was riveted on this historic moment. Iran looked to be changing for the better. There was a strong sense of renewed hope for a people long stifled. It was a pivotal time in Iran, and just as five years earlier I had felt a strong pull to go to America, I now felt that same strong urge to return to Iran. It was a patriotic urge; I was proud of my country and longed to be part of its reshaping.

On a rainy evening in January 1979, I met with Soroosh and Asghar, friends from my MBA program. We sat in a coffee shop in Fort Lauderdale and excitedly talked about what was happening in Iran.

"Can you believe it?" Soroosh asked. "The Shah has fled the country!"

"That's crazy," Asghar said. "I never thought I'd live to see the day."

"Me neither." I eyed my friends closely. "Have you ever thought about going back?"

"Going back?" Asghar said. "When? Now?" He gave me a look like: You have to be kidding me!

I shrugged. "Why not? Don't you want to see what's happening up close? Don't you want to be part of the revolution?"

"Not if it's going to get me killed!" Asghar laughed.

"Quit being so dramatic." I said. "You're not going to get killed. Don't you see the opportunity for us?"

"Opportunity for what?" Soroosh looked puzzled, and I could understand why. We had never learned to put "Iran" and "opportunity" in the same sentence.

"I don't know. To be part of the restructuring of businesses there," I said. "The economy is struggling—businesses are collapsing. Maybe we have the expertise to help them rebuild."

"Are you serious?" Soroosh said.

"Dead serious."

"So, what are you saying?" Asghar asked. He seemed intrigued, but Soroosh looked far from convinced.

"I'm saying people like us—who have MBAs, who have the management and business know-how—we could really make a difference in Iran right now."

We talked this over the rest of that night and returned to the conversation the following week. I was eager to share my plan to form a consulting company and offer our business services to leadership in Tehran corporations. Soroosh was an industrial engineer. Asghar was an accountant. I had an MBA with a major in finance and was working on my DBA. Together, we could offer a wealth of business expertise. After another week of deliberation, Asghar and I had won. We started making our plans to move forward.

In all honesty, I had already decided I was going back to Iran whether they came or not. Nothing could hold me back.

The next month, I met with my advisor at Nova University to tell him my plans to take a leave of absence.

He looked at me with concern. "Are you sure this is a good idea, Mehdi? This is just your first year here. It could be dangerous to disrupt your progress."

I stifled a small chuckle. Dangerous to disrupt my studies? Not nearly as dangerous as returning to a country that has gone through—was still going through—a massive upheaval, with one leader and form of government ousted as they prepared to be replaced by a new leader and another form of government. "Iran is my home country," I answered. "I need to go back to help in any way I can."

"Quite often, when a student takes leave, they don't return—even if they intend to," he said. "Life gets in the way. Do you want to risk that?"

"I came to America to get a college education," I replied. My shoulders felt tense from my rigid stance. "I have a bachelor's and a master's degree. And now I'm working on my doctorate. I am still determined to get my doctoral degree, but I can't ignore what's going on in Iran. I just need to go back for a while, and then I'll return to finish the program."

Hearing my determination, he sighed and handed me the forms to fill out and submit for my leave of absence. In a matter of days, the three of us were on an Iran Air flight from JFK to Tehran.

My brother Ali picked me up at the airport, just as nearly five years earlier he had dropped me off. Asghar and Soroosh, who were picked up by their relatives, had agreed to meet me in a few days. Although it was nine in the evening, I felt awake, my senses sharpened and adrenaline coursing through my veins. I could sense an eager anticipation amongst my fellow travelers. There was electricity in the air. I was exacerbated by seeing armed soldiers patrolling the building.

I'm not sure what I expected to come home to. After all, the country was in disarray. Although the Shah had been deposed, a country can't magically transform itself in a month. It was like returning to the aftermath of an earthquake, with the ever-present danger of aftershocks.

As I tossed my suitcase into Ali's trunk, I could see he'd aged. There was a subtle thinning of his once-dark hair. His eyes seemed tired. I'm sure he was thinking the same about me.

"You're looking good," I said as we drove off.

"You never were a good liar," he scoffed. We laughed together.

"So, you came back to see what's happening in Iran, eh?" he said as he pulled up to the stoplight

"I wanted to see what's happening here—experience it for myself, with my own eyes."

Ali slowly pulled the car forward as the light changed. "If you want to know the truth—and you'll see it soon enough for yourself—the country is in chaos. Khomeini's government is trying to take charge and bring back order. You saw the armed guards at the airport? They're everywhere."

"Yeah, they were hard to miss."

I was disheartened. Of course, things were turbulent. Ali told me that martial law was in effect, and no one could be on the streets after eight o'clock at night.

"The guards are everywhere you go, not just at the airport," he said. "They have machine guns hanging from their shoulders and grenades in their pockets. Ayatollah Khomeini dismantled the old military and police. He created a revolutionary guard and a new military force called Sepha. It's a war zone, Mehdi." He kept his eyes on the road. They looked deadened to me, like someone who was suffering from battle fatigue.

We drove in silence as I digested his news.

"How's Dad?" I finally asked.

"Dad is in a good neighborhood. His business is doing well, actually. And he's anxious to see you."

The neighborhood was, indeed, nicer. With the price of real estate plummeting, Dad bought a four-level condominium with a first-story garage in the northern part of Tehran. He lived in one unit. The other units were designated for two of his children—my brother, Ahmad, and myself. He hoped I would finish my doctorate, move home, and marry a "nice Iranian girl."

That night, my siblings came over for a party. We ate my stepmother's traditional Iranian dishes and we talked late into the night. Everyone wanted to know about life in America. They were fascinated by my summer trip across the United States, pointing in excitement at my photographs of the Arizona mountains, the Golden Gate Bridge, and beaches in San Diego.

"We drove over 8,000 miles, Dad," I said as he flipped through the photos.

His jaw dropped. "No way."

"It's true. America's a big country."

Over lamb kebabs and saffron rice cakes, he told me how his business had picked up. Now, he owned his own shop. No partner! My brother-in-law, an accountant, helped him expand the store by buying the adjacent shop. He looked tired but good.

Me in Tehran, Iran during my visit in 1979

None of my 10 siblings had to drop out before graduating high school. Conversely, none of them went to college either. Interesting that I was the only one who dropped out of school—and the only one to earn additional degrees, including my doctorate.

"Are you working a lot?" I asked, knowing the answer.

He just shrugged.

"He's never not working," Ali chimed in. "He gets up at five every morning of the week to work. And he doesn't come home until it is time to go to bed. You should consider yourself lucky that he's not working right now."

"Special occasion," my father grinned.

We finally went to bed. I slept in the unit that Dad had saved especially for me to come back and live in. He'd bought a small bed that looked inviting. Although exhausted, as soon as I lay down, my mind started racing with thoughts and worry. It felt strange (in a good way) to be back home, and I didn't know how long I'd stay. Just as with the country itself, everything was up in the air for me. The soft sheets and warm blankets seemed to mock my inability to switch off.

Picture of my father during my visit to Tehran, Iran in 1979. He was 52 years old then.

In a few days, I reunited with Soroosh and Asghar in a local coffee shop.

"With the Shah gone, things should soon be opening up," I said. "Have you seen what's happened to so many industries here? The revolutionaries have taken them over, and the owners have fled or were put behind bars! And the people now in charge of these businesses—they don't know how to run a business."

It all sounded good—in theory.

For six months, we tried to get our consulting business off the ground, facing a myriad of barriers when trying to schedule meetings. When we did manage a meeting, the company managers had little knowledge about business operations. From across the table, they'd stare at us stone-faced, occasionally grunting. They rarely asked questions. Then, they'd tell us they weren't interested in any help. Our insight continued to fall on deaf ears. It made me wonder why they took the meeting in the first place. It was very frustrating.

Like our meeting back in Fort Lauderdale in January, Asghar, Soroosh, and I met in a Tehran coffee shop in August. We all quickly came to the same conclusion: Our idea of helping our society get back on its feet, of providing wise counsel to corporations in the midst of all the change going on, had fallen flatter than a pancake. Life was still a struggle in Iran, and, in many ways, we felt like we didn't belong.

"Maybe it's time to go back to the U.S.," I said. Neither Soroosh nor Asghar balked at the idea.

It was settled. I renewed my visa, said goodbye to my family, and booked a flight back to Miami. I resumed my doctoral program in September 1979.

I struggled with disappointment on my flight back. While I was happy to see my family, especially my dad, the country was still in chaos and our plan had failed. I felt defeated. I had truly wanted to make things work in Iran, but the timing and the circumstances were wrong.

As I gazed out the plane window, Miami gradually came into focus, and a sense of calm replaced my earlier sullenness. At this moment, I realized that the United States, with its open doors and bright hopes, was now my home. Optimism washed over me and the funk I had been in just evaporated—just like an early morning fog dissipating in the sun. I felt a renewed energy and enthusiasm, eager to embrace the next steps in my journey.

Something had been confirmed in me over those six months in Iran, especially on the flight across the Atlantic.

I wasn't just returning to America.

I was coming home.

The next day, after I returned to Fort Lauderdale, I made an appointment with my doctoral advisor, Dr. Novak, to discuss my plans to return. I'd missed almost a year of the program; therefore, I needed to accelerate my efforts, taking a full course load each semester plus summer courses to complete the 48 credit hours of required courses before I could sit for the comprehensive exam.

At the end of the summer of 1980, I took the eight-hour written exam, passing with an A. I immediately followed up with Dr. Novak to begin the process of my doctoral dissertation. He was very pleased to hear about my progress

"Mehdi, I'm so impressed to see how quickly you made up for your lost year. Your hard work and determination are paying off." Then, he asked me to begin my scholarly research to identify my dissertation topic and goal. We agreed on a plan to complete my dissertation in 18 months.

After several weeks of extensive library research, I returned to Dr. Novak with my decision to focus on management information systems (MIS) and strategic decision making in organizations. During the 1980s, the concept of managing information as a major resource, similar to human resources, financial resources, and physical resources, became very popular and powerful in organizations. As a result, the concept of MIS was invented, encompassing all aspects of information resources management within an organization. My dissertation aimed to determine the impact of MIS on the strategic process of major organizations and to learn how these organizations use information resources to enhance their processes and outcomes.

To complete my comprehensive research, I needed to familiarize myself with concepts and practices within MIS. I visited local universities that offered robust graduate programs in MIS, finding that my alma mater, the University of Miami, was the highest-ranked institution. I called the school's graduate admission program and, a week later, met Ms. Meledy Johnson, a graduate admissions advisor.

I expressed my interest in taking a few graduate courses in their computer information systems (CIS) program, but she convinced me that I'd be better off enrolling in their graduate CIS engineering program with a Master of Science in CIS engineering. She reviewed my transcripts for my MBA and DBA programs, finding that at least 12 credit hours could be transferred, with an additional 24 credit hours required to complete the program.

By the fall of 1980, I had started my second master's degree program at the University of Miami. The initial application for the program asked if I had an interest in scholarship or teaching assistance programs, for which I checked the "yes" box. Surprisingly, a week after the semester began, I received a letter from the dean of the graduate school with an offer for a full scholarship based on my prior grades, as well as my knowledge of computer programming. The scholarship provided my tuition and a US$300 monthly stipend in return for on-the-job training.

I had worked a number of jobs—busboy, valet, waiter—to support myself and fund my education in the four years since I had come to America. Anything to keep the money flowing (or at least a steady trickle to keep me afloat). So, I did what I always did—opened the Sunday edition of the Miami Herald and began circling jobs in the want ads section of the newspaper.

I found that my education—both my bachelor's and my pending MBA—qualified me for a lot of positions. Even my work toward my associate's degree at Miami–Dade Community College opened potential doors. In this case, it was a critical piece in my getting my first "real world" job.

Through my newspaper search, I secured an interview with Systems Engineering Laboratories in Fort Lauderdale. About 10 years earlier, the company had been involved in the breakout of minicomputers, from 16-bit to larger architectures. One of the interviewers, Professor Raymond Van Heerden, worked in the school's Department of Finance. He asked me to tell him about my life and academic path.

"You had to quit school at 14?" the professor asked, leaning back in his chair.

"Yes," I said. "I had to help my father support my family."

"And you came to America knowing how much English?" he asked.

"I knew about 10 words." I said. "I learned quickly how to say 'McDonald's.'"

The professor laughed.

"It's remarkable," he said. "You quit school, went on to earn many degrees, and now you are in your doctoral program and pursuing your second master's degree. Very good."

I smiled. "Once I have a goal in mind, I don't let go."

Professor Van Heerden was developing a massive software program for financial predictions. The next day, Systems Engineering Laboratories offered me an (unpaid) internship, serving as one of six FORTRAN programmers. I knew the experience would look good on a resume, potentially leading to a paid, full-time position after graduation. I was eager to accept the opportunity and reported to work the next day.

I dedicated myself to my new role, working at least 20 hours throughout the week and on weekends to meet Professor Van Heerden's expectations. We developed a mutually respectful relationship. He appreciated my commitment. I valued his guidance. Whenever I needed time to study, he was understanding and made sure I had the flexibility to balance my academic responsibilities. I quickly became his point man as a programmer—if he gave me a task, I completed the job. And if any parts of the project were behind schedule, I was the guy who could fix it. Sometimes, he'd ask me to stop by the dry cleaners on the way to work to pick up his suits. Then, he'd reciprocate by giving me a half day off if I needed to get something done. For example, if I had a dentist appointment in the late morning, he'd tell me to take the rest of the day off. Above all, it was a positive and productive environment in which I gained exceptional experience in computer programming, system analysis, and software development.

I had taken several elective programming courses at Miami–Dade and the University of Miami to deepen my fluency in programming languages like BASIC, FORTRAN, and COBOL. I also explored statistical software packages like SAS and SPSS. I was excited about the scholarship work opportunity because it would let me learn more about the latest tech evolutions in the world of computing. (Now, more than 40 years later, technological changes have ramped up at a dizzying speed, making computing in the late 1970s seem very pedantic in comparison!)

Developing an executable computer program that solves problems or computerizes a task requires multiple steps. Here's how archaic computer programming was back in the day: First, a programmer had to write the code in their chosen programming language. Then, the lines of code were transferred onto rectangular punch cards and fed into large IBM 1402 card reader machines. Sometimes, the entire code for a project would require several thousand cards, which the programmer would painstakingly run through the readers at the computer center.

My Iranian friend at the University of Miami, Naser, was one of the best COBOL programmers I'd ever met. He seemed to have the Midas touch; his programs never failed. One day I asked him, "How did you get so good at this? What's your secret?"

He gave a low laugh that sounded more like a snort of amusement. "Back in Iran, the college I attended couldn't afford an IBM computer with a card reader. It could barely afford desks and chairs for the students! So, I had to learn programming without a computer."

I furrowed my brow. "Without a computer? How could you even do that?"

Naser smiled. "It was grueling. There were many times when I wanted to just give up. But my professor said, 'We don't have computers. So, you will function as the computer. Just think—if you do well without a computer, wait to see how good you are with one!'"

"Oh my gosh! That sounds like torture," I said.

"It was. We would write our code and submit it to our professor to correct any mistakes. We learned the hard way, believe me." Naser winked. "But sometimes, when you learn the hard way, it sticks with you. Then, the easy way becomes very easy."

I'll never forget that conversation or the lesson that I learned. Naser faced a severe limitation, one that directly and greatly inhibited his goal of becoming a programmer. A very common and understandable response to that would be to give up and pursue a different path. Still, he never lost sight of his goal, leveraging his resource limitation into an advantage. The most inspiring stories aren't about those with ample resources, support, and advantages. They are the stories of those who faced significant disadvantages—and made something of themselves despite all of that.

I have immense respect for Naser, who met challenges head-on with determination. Hearing about his approach, I reflected on my own methods for tackling adversity. It was like when I had to drop out of school and work full-time. I could have given up my education dream. Instead, I attained my GED and made sacrifices to continue my studies in the United States. Like him, I aimed to confront barriers with a blend of innovation and hard work. I was encouraged to see those qualities mirrored in someone else.

I also began working approximately 10 hours a week with Professor Efraim Turban, a professor of management science from Tel Aviv University who was spending two years in Miami. He was well-known in his field and had authored many books and journal articles. We met at his office, where he outlined the graduate-level courses he was teaching. He told me that he had already reviewed my resume and knew all about my educational background. He was a very serious man, rarely smiling, and very direct (and no sense of humor at all). I was scheduled to assist him with two course sections on regression analysis, filling in for him when he was unavailable to teach and helping with exam preparation and grading. I was simultaneously nervous and excited at the notion of teaching a graduate-level class, which I had never done, but I was thrilled about the prospect of working with such a reputable professor and researcher.

"Thank you for the opportunity, Professor Turban," I said. "I will do my best to assist you in any way that I can."

"I don't expect anything less," he responded with a robust Israeli accent.

Throughout the fall of 1980, I was a full-time graduate student at the University of Miami, working up to 60 hours a week between the two professors, as well as preparing my doctoral dissertation project full-time at Nova Southeastern University. My weekends were also dedicated to working as a night security guard because the US$300 a month stipend was not enough to survive.

After the fall semester at the University of Miami and teaching for Professor Turban, I found that teaching was an enjoyable challenge, presenting opportunities to engage with motivated students on complex topics. I started looking around for college-level teaching opportunities. In the spring semester of 1981, I picked up several teaching positions: an early morning undergraduate course in operational research on Tuesdays and Thursday at Florida International University, a COBOL programming course at Broward Community College, and a course in the principles of data processing at West Palm Beach, Broward Community College. I taught both courses at Broward in the evenings, Monday through Friday. During the week, I'd leave my condo at six o'clock in the morning and return 14 hours later. On the weekend, I'd work a full shift in security, using the remainder of each evening to study at the nearby library.

In all, I was dedicating more than 90 hours a week to my educational programs and work. My life was consumed by work and studies, leaving little room for anything else. Every day was carefully planned, filled with hours of lectures, assignments, and responsibilities. These were the necessary steps I had to take because I was always looking forward, planning for my next milestone. It was exhausting, but it was essential.

I ended up working for Systems Engineering Laboratories for about a year and a half. Once I finished my MBA, the company paid me for my work. Professor Van Heerden tried to convince me to stay at the company, even offering to sponsor my visa. Although the offer was tempting, my gut was telling me that it was time to move on. The job wasn't bad, but I wanted more. I didn't come to America and get my degrees to become a computer programmer.

Now, I had—in comparison to my first years in America—some financial security. With my education, I was prepared to pursue the next stage of my career. I was no longer aiming to satisfy my visa requirements or simply earn enough money to pay tuition. These subsequent steps would be strategic and measured.

"A mind is a terrible thing to waste."

I wanted to move on from programming—but to what? I engaged in some prolonged introspection as I mulled over my options. I clearly remember watching the PSA for the United Negro College Fund, the brainchild of its executive director Arthur Fletcher, to promote equal education and elevation for all Americans. The compelling campaign lasted decades, illustrating the different destinies of Black children who attended college and those who did not.

Advertisers aimed the messaging at underserved kids who were the first in their families to attend college. Though I wasn't a part of the target audience, its message resonated with me. I, too, did not want to waste my mind or any experiences in "the land of opportunity."

"Once you've attained your doctoral degree, you have reached the very top," a professor once told me.

While I silently agreed with the professor, his statement didn't have a life-changing impact on me at the time. I returned to that statement, giving it more serious thought. With my MBA, I had a degree that was tied to specific types of careers. Did I really need a doctoral degree? Would I regret not reaching the educational pinnacle? Would stopping at a master's degree feel like I had been climbing Mt. Everest only to turn at the final camp before ascending to the top?

I reflected on my journey, which began at age 14 when I was forced to quit school and work full-time to help support my family. I had gone to night school to get my GED. Against all odds, I came to America knowing only a handful of words, determined to continue my studies. I had supported both myself and my education by working long hours at low-paying jobs, even as I took on full course loads and completed my degrees early. I earned my associate's degree, my bachelor's degree, and my first MBA. Now, I was working on my second master's degree and completing my doctoral dissertation in lab technology.

For many people, especially those who grew up in Iran when I did, college wasn't even a pipe dream. I was the first and only member of my family to attend college, much less earn what would eventually be five degrees. I'd embraced the American culture, including the slang and idioms. I was like that little black fish—a long way from home. And my life was all the richer for it.

I was undoubtedly grateful for the lab job and all the opportunities I'd had in America, both with work and education. But the more I thought about it, the more unwavering I was to finishing climbing that educational peak. I was going to go to the summit—the doctoral degree. I had come to America to get an education, and I wasn't going to stop until I reached the pinnacle.

By the end of that summer, I'd finished my graduate course requirements and received my Master of Science in CIS from Miami. I was enrolled in the doctoral program at Nova when I accepted a full-time teaching position from the chair, Professor Ted Stevens, at the Broward Community College Department of Data Processing in Fort Lauderdale. I began teaching five courses each semester beginning in September while completing my doctoral dissertation. I also taught two courses—one on management science at Florida International University and another in data processing at Broward Community College, Palm Beach—and worked as a weekend security guard. It was a 90-hour workweek, but I had no intention of slowing down.

Dad used to say, "There are times in your life that you can run, and you better run. And there will be times that you want to run, but you cannot!" In 1981, I was running as fast and as far as I could!

The following summer, after a painstaking process of collecting and analyzing data, validating my hypothesis, and writing a 269-page essay, I submitted my dissertation to Professor Novak. He then submitted it to my dissertation committee. Eventually, I appeared in front of the committee to defend my case. It appeared that the members of the committee held a respectful regard for my work. They provided constructive feedback, acknowledged the significance of my research, and engaged with me in meaningful dialogue. I left with only a few areas to address prior to my next submission.

In May 1982, I received an official letter from the Nova Southeastern University Graduate School stating that I had fulfilled all course requirements for the DBA. I'd successfully passed the written exam and completed my dissertation. As a result, I was set to be awarded a DBA with a major in information systems.

The day I received this letter, I began flying in the clouds for many days! I'd finally done it—I'd reached the pinnacle of my education journey!

References

Mottahedeh, R. P. (1985). *The mantle of the prophet*. Oneworld Publications.

Graduation Commencement receiving my doctorate degree at Nova Southeastern University, July 1982

Chapter 8
My Academic Career

Six months prior to completing my doctoral degree, I had started submitting applications to the academic job market, mailing out more than 200 copies of my resume to reputable colleges and universities throughout the United States. Three schools responded very positively to my application: Ball State University in Indiana, Bentley College in Boston, and Pennsylvania State University. I was invited to visit each campus and meet with their faculty and deans—a common practice during the interview process. In doing so, I was able to learn more about their academic programs and settings. In turn, they could also learn more about me through long interviews and meetings with key decision-makers within each institution.

By April 1982, after extensive discussions with my advisor, Dr. Novak, I accepted the offer from Pennsylvania State University's Harrisburg campus. Not only was Penn State a reputable institution, but it was also one of the largest landmark universities in the country. It had a rich history, distinguished programs, and active community engagement. Dr. Novak believed that joining the institution was like joining IBM in the corporate world.

I stepped into my instructor role with the Penn State University Department of CIS in July 1982. I had accepted the offer to work at its School of Business Administration while still in the process of completing my doctoral degree program. At the time I accepted the job offer, my doctoral degree was ABD (all but dissertation), a title given to doctoral students when they reach a point in their program in which they have finished their course requirements but must still complete their dissertation.

Within a year, Penn State recognized my contributions and dedication, elevating me from an instructor to a tenure-track position as an assistant professor of CIS. This rapid advancement validated my commitment to academia and gave me opportunities to contribute to my profession.

My first academic post came with an annual salary of US$28,500—with a bachelor's degree, two master's degrees, and a doctoral degree. To put this into perspective, in the early 1980s, a corporate job requiring only a bachelor's degree in business offered an annual salary of US$25,000. Ten years later, as a tenured faculty member and program chair, my annual salary had increased to US$33,500.

Needless to say, I didn't stay in academia for the salary or the prestige alone. I was driven by a deeper passion for knowledge dissemination and academic research. I used the role to further my educational mission, relishing the tremendous joy of teaching. Now that I had achieved my childhood dreams, I wanted to become an educational ambassador, hoping to share that gift with younger generations.

At 31 years old, I was one of the younger faculty members in the School of Business Administration. There were 30 full-time professors in the school, averaging 60 years of age. Many of my students found me approachable, talking to me about their lives, their ambitions, and their difficulties. Sometimes, I would hang out with them after school, meeting up at a local lounge for drinks or dinner.

At the University of Miami, I never had time to attend the school's football games to rally behind the Hurricanes. I was too involved in class, my studies, and work. However, at Penn State, following the Nittany Lions was like a religion. I attended almost all the homecoming games at the main campus in State College, learning quickly to love tailgating with grilled hot dogs and cold beer.

My move to Middletown was a major adjustment. The tiny town was nestled along the Susquehanna River, about 10 miles from Pennsylvania's capital city of Harrisburg. I'd found Melbourne to be small when I lived there in 1978. Still, its proximity to the Kennedy Space Center, Disney World, and Harris Corporation made it feel huge compared to Middletown. My new hometown lacked the glitz and glamour of South Florida—no more nightclubs with pulsating music or panoramic views from trendy rooftop restaurants. Numbering about 1,000 residents, Middletown's two roads went east to west and south to north. Each evening, the streetlights dimmed at eight, businesses shuttered their doors, and the town got quiet. It transformed into a ghost town, and it was hard to get used to the new pace. I told my friends in Miami that the only place I could party after dark was the cemetery, a few blocks from my two-bedroom apartment.

In Iranian culture, living near a cemetery was taboo, reserved only for the poor and unfortunate. Despite this cultural difference, Pennsylvania felt reminiscent of Tehran's four-season climate, with frigid winters, hot and humid summers, and lovely transitional fall and spring seasons.

I also had to adjust to the small-town mentality and issues with stereotyping. Within the first week of arriving, I went to a local bank, Commonwealth National, to open a checking account and establish a direct deposit from my new employer. A bank representative greeted me and asked for my driver's license to begin filling out the application. I handed her my Florida identification and told her I'd just started my job at Penn State.

"So, you're a driver with the university?" she asked as she began writing down my position in the paperwork.

"No, not a driver," I replied. "I'm a professor."

She apologized for having possibly insulted me, but I reassured her it was fine. After we completed the paperwork, I asked her why she thought I was a driver. I assumed it was because I was an immigrant with an accent.

"Oh, your driver's license said chauffeur class instead of operator," she replied. That made sense. To drive limousines for VIP guests at Miami's Fontainebleau, I had to obtain a professional class driver's license—the chauffeur class. Typically, people secure an operator class to drive personal cars. Obviously, the woman at the bank saw the chauffeur designation and made a logical assumption about my new job at Penn State University.

In Middletown, everyone seemed to know each other and everything you did. In the tight-knit community, neighbors greeted each other by name and local businesses recognized their patrons. One afternoon that summer, I rushed to get to the town's post office before it closed. In fact, I was probably driving faster than the 35-mile-per-hour speed limit. Then, the following morning, when I went to fill out forms at the school's Office of Human Resources, the head of the department asked me if I drove a brown Toyota Celica.

"Yes, I do. Why?" I asked.

"Because I saw you speeding through town yesterday," her gaze was fixed on me. My jaw dropped with her observation. I realized then that I needed to be very careful about my personal life, as it became clear that privacy was non-existent in this small town.

At 31 years old, I was teaching a mix of classes on data structures, telecommunications, database design, systems analysis, MIS, and statistics in the Department of CIS within the university's School of Business. I was also leading computer language programming courses, including COBOL programming and FORTRAN programming.

Six months into my tenure, the dean of the School of Business, Professor Larry Geelman, summoned me into his office. He had started his career as an army colonel and, once retired, obtained his doctoral degree and joined the Penn State faculty. Everything from his mannerisms to his haircut was precise.

As a military man myself, I greeted the dean with a respectful indoor salute, a gesture that demonstrated my respect for his service and our shared commitment to discipline. He nodded, inviting me to take a seat, and explained that the current chair of the Department of CIS was leaving for a 12-month sabbatical to complete her doctoral degree. In the interim, he needed to appoint a new chair to the department. Based on his observation of my work ethic and commitment to the job, he "thought I was the best candidate for the role."

The offer came as a surprise. He'd passed over many of my senior colleagues, one of whom had been on the faculty for seven years, had a PhD from Harvard, and was keen on becoming chair himself.

Professor Geelman called me "an eagle." He saw me arrive on campus each morning at eight, often staying until 11 at night. He had run into me on the weekends, long after everyone else had departed. He saw my determination to succeed and lead without hesitation. I happily accepted his offer.

Over my 14-year stint as department chair, I changed the department's architecture to increase efficiency, attract new talent, and incorporate sustainability principles. I also developed new course offerings, including a Master of Science in Information Systems graduate degree.

Before I had accepted my faculty position at Penn State in 1982, I was dating Rachel. We'd met while I was a doctoral student in Florida, serving as a security guard at a condominium complex clubhouse in Hollywood. Rachel, a British au pair, was living with a family in the complex and often brought the children to the clubhouse. We began dating in 1981 and, once she completed her au pair assignment, we moved in together.

A year later, after careful consideration and weighing my options, I made the decision to relocate to Pennsylvania for my new job opportunity. Although Rachel returned to England to live with her parents in Oxfordshire, we stayed in touch, and she eventually returned to the States. I proposed to her just before Thanksgiving in 1982. We had a small ceremony officiated by Middletown's Justice of the Peace. My cousin, Farhad, attended, as did Ali, my college friend, and my Penn State colleague, Professor Jasim.

On the day of our wedding, my secretary, Louise, burst into my office, arms flailing. "Mehdi, it's time to go to the Justice of the Peace—you're getting married today!" As I stood up from my desk, I could hear her muttering in exasperation, "You've got to be kidding me."

I was driven by my work, yet I often found myself immersed in deadlines and tasks. Despite the stress, I genuinely enjoyed its pace. The satisfaction of achieving goals and the pride I had in my projects kept me going, even though it could lead to an imbalance in my life.

Even on Christmas Day, just a month into my marriage, I went into the office to catch up on my upcoming course preparation and accumulation of papers. In the early 1980s, there were neither personal computers nor remote work options. You needed to be physically in an office to connect your computer to a hardline internet connection in the wall. Rachel was at home, cooking our first Christmas meal. She expressed her displeasure with my decision to go to work, but I assured her I would be home in time for the festivities. I just "needed to get some work done first."

When I arrived at my university office that morning, my key didn't work. I'd forgotten that the maintenance office had changed the lock on all the entrance doors. Obviously, my key was for the old lock. The only way I could get into the building was to have the school's security officer unlock it. When I approached the on-duty officers, I identified myself as a member of the faculty in the School of Business.

"Today's Christmas, professor," the head officer replied. "You should be home with your family." While I appreciated his recommendation, I still needed to get into my office. He persisted, denying me access.

"I don't need a lecture," I said tensely. "I'm a faculty member, and I just need entry to my office."

He was adamant in his refusal to open the door on a holiday, so I called my dean, Professor Geelman. After I explained my concern to him, he spoke to the head of security. Soon, I was walking through the front door after the officer finally unlocked it. As it swung open, he shot me a look of disapproval.

By the time I finished my work and returned home to Rachel, it was eight o'clock at night. Despite the joyful holiday season, she was not at all happy!

In addition to teaching my regular classes and chairing the department, I began teaching two three-credit courses in computer programming for the university's Department of Continuing Education. I was paid an additional US$1,500 for each. Individuals who were not enrolled in the school's traditional degree program could sign up for these courses to earn a general certification in computer programming. Because of the university's location near the state's capital, many of my non-traditional students were government employees.

Soon, I developed a full certificate program in CIS for non-traditional students. Upon completion of the course requirements, the students would receive a certificate diploma from the university. The new program consisted of nine three-credit courses, with students taking a minimum of six courses, including the required curriculum and electives. The program was accepted by the Department of Continuing Education, and in January 1983, it opened to the public. I was not surprised at the program's success in generating more than US$100,000 in its first year, given the high demand and uniqueness of its offerings. It addressed a gap in the market by providing education that was embraced by its audience. Thus, it led to an impressive performance.

I continued teaching two courses throughout the spring, fall, and summer semesters. Again, each course paid US$1,500. I also earned US$1,500 for serving as the academic coordinator of the certificate program. On average, I was making an additional US$10,000 a year from my roles with the Department of Continuing Education.

Furthermore, I began receiving calls from local business leaders seeking motivated faculty or students skilled in computer programming or systems development. This inspired me to create a comprehensive internship program, allowing our students to engage in real-world job opportunities while earning valuable experience and credit hours toward the completion of their degree. To further address the gaps in industry needs, I also designed a consulting company offering computer system–related services. I began accepting clients from the business community for various jobs totaling US$20,000 in additional income. This brought my total annual income to nearly US$60,000.

As my various streams of income began to add up, I felt a sense of momentum building in my career. Each opportunity I pursued seemed to complement the others, creating a synergy that propelled me forward. The sense of excitement and anticipation filled me with confidence, knowing that I was on my path to realizing my full potential.

Nearly everyone, including my own secretary, referred to me as "Dr. K" because they had difficulty pronouncing my last name. From the hallways, students would call out, "Hey, Dr. K."

I averaged 16 hours per day on campus preparing my course materials, chairing the department, advising students, and conducting my research to publish in scholarly journals, a requirement of my appointment as a tenure-track faculty member.

In academia, a tenure-track position is awarded if the faculty member meets the university's annual requirements in teaching, research, and service, such as committee and taskforce participation, for six consecutive years. Once they meet tenure, the individual is "awarded" a tenure status, meaning they can maintain their faculty position for life at the same institution. This is considered one of the most valued perks of working at a research-based institution like Penn State.

While I could be friendly with my students, I also had a reputation for being one of the toughest professors. When I assumed the chair position, I was assigned several of the former chair's courses, including "Introduction to COBOL Programming Language." On the first night of class, I outlined my expectations of the students and distributed the course syllabus, including 12 programming assignments and three exams. More than 10 of the 27 students failed to return to the classroom after the evening's first restroom break. I later discovered that the former chair's syllabus included three programming assignments and two exams—quite a difference from my criteria!

As the course ended, the remaining students' conclusion survey stated that they felt a sense of achievement, were challenged by the rigorous materials, and believed they were gaining long-term benefits. I was motivated to continue with my policy of maintaining high expectations. I aimed to push and challenge students to ensure they were well-prepared for the job market, capable of securing high-quality employment and success in their careers.

My courses were often technical, covering topics like data structures, algorithms, and models for developing programs that would allow compilers like COBOL to convert machine languages or binary languages for execution on the computer. Given that the students were tackling courses that were complex and intense, I tried to start each class with a joke and build two breaks into the nearly three-hour class period.

Throughout my tenure at Penn State, I received several university awards, including the James A. Jordan Award for Teaching Excellence. While awards and accolades recognized my professional work, what moved me was the feedback from students and the opportunity to see them flourish. Celebrating their milestones and achievements and witnessing the impact of our collective efforts was incredibly rewarding (perhaps my favorite and most important part of the job).

As mentioned, faculty members with tenure-track appointments are required to teach, perform research, and participate in service activities. The students and my love for teaching kept me at Penn State for nearly 19 years. In addition, the fields of computer science and information technology were evolving at a rapid pace, and scholarly research allowed me to play a role in discovering fascinating frontiers in emerging technologies. Through my service commitments, however, I witnessed the play of internal politics that negatively impacted the livelihood of my colleagues. And I was hired to teach and conduct research—not play politics!

"Academic politics are so vicious because the stakes are so small." This quote—or a version of it—has been attributed to many people, including California politician Jesse Unruh and American scholar-turned-diplomat Henry Kissinger. Whatever its origin, it captures the essence of many fields, including academia. Admittedly, politics forms in all fields, whether it be the corporate world, government, non-profits, or the religious sector. Internal conflicts and power struggles can be difficult to navigate and may even derail one's career. In academia, I routinely observed and experienced competition and contention that was more intense than in any other domain in which I have operated.

One significant factor that exacerbated academic struggles was ego. A sense of self-importance would hinder individuals from seeking help, acknowledging a weakness, or collaborating with others. Faculty members have earned the highest level of education, and because they have students refer to them deferentially, they tend to hold themselves in high regard. Faculty meetings were often stocked with dozens of egos, all unable to agree on a single topic. For several hours, insults and arguments were fired back and forth—but nothing would get done.

Five years into my tenure as department chair, I attended a faculty meeting on standard agenda items and routine department business. Suddenly, the discussion veered into the development of marketing materials to increase student applications to the new MBA program. Somewhere between student recruitment and curricula development, a member of the faculty suggested using the word "enrichment" to effectively demonstrate our goals. This recommendation, while it may sound innocent, led to a heated debate. Some faculty agreed that the word should be featured in promotional materials, while other members argued vehemently that the term "advancement" better captured the nuance of the MBA strategy.

"Who cares?" I kept thinking. Potential recruits receiving the marketing literature wouldn't even notice these words. Their decision to matriculate would center on faculty qualifications, the quality of students' experiences, and the program's post-graduation job-placement records.

After hours of arguments and shouting, the faculty could not agree on a word and the meeting ended without a decision.

At other moments, too, the pettiness reached embarrassing lows. One of the school's talented professors of marketing, with a great publication record and healthy ego, strongly disliked an equally accomplished and proud professor of finance. Their mutual animosity was apparent to everyone and could instantly sour the mood of a meeting. One day, after a bitter disagreement about something trivial, one of these scholars entered the department after hours, dislodged the other scholar's nametag from his office door, and affixed it to the door of the men's restroom.

Once I received tenure at Penn State, my presence and opinions began to carry significantly more weight. While this status afforded me some greater influence and respect among my colleagues, I also noticed an escalation within the in-group vs. out-group dynamic. Individuals aligned themselves over topics like faculty and administrative appointments, research methodologies, and political ideologies. This divisive behavior overshadowed compromise and the common good. As my commitments increased, I imagined what it would be like to do the impossible: leave my tenure role.

I made a concerted effort to insulate myself from these childlike antics, using different strategies to maintain focus and professionalism. I sought to avoid unnecessary interactions or distractions. Often, I would even close my office door—in violation of my own open-door policy—to avoid my colleagues' petty complaints. Despite my efforts to drown out the noise, someone would inevitably knock to ask, "Do you have a minute?" After smiling and offering them a seat, they would launch into what, by academic standards, was a major injustice: a colleague's travel reimbursement, the smell of someone's lunch in the break room, or the temperature of the office.

The complaints could drag on for hours.

Despite their high level of education, many of my colleagues exhibited a surprising resistance to change and process improvement. This reluctance persisted even when presented with clear evidence and logical arguments demonstrating the benefits of adopting new technologies or techniques. I was intrigued to see such knowledgeable people cling to outdated methods, often preferring the comfort of routine over the potential benefit of a new approach.

For instance, after joining the university's CIS program, I noticed its curriculum lacked a course in database principles and management, a common course I taught at Broward Community College. I prepared the CIS course materials and submitted them to the dean of the School of Business, who would then share them with various committees within the school, the college, and the university. I attended the School of Business Committee for Curriculum Improvement meeting to outline the proposed course, as well as its impact on students' knowledge of database principles and practices. To my surprise, my colleagues did not ask constructive questions or support my efforts to address a significant shortcoming within our curriculum. Instead of engaging with the merits of the proposal, my colleagues launched a personal attack. In fact, a faculty member in the marketing field questioned the substance of the course even though the subject was outside his area of expertise.

I was taken aback by their level of resistance after I had invested time in preparing an extensive proposal and offered to teach the course. After two hours of debate and discussion, during which many perspectives and concerns were examined, the proposal was finally approved by the committee. Yet, it felt less like a professional discussion and more like an onslaught of criticism directed at me as an individual rather than the idea itself.

Regrettably, this hostile and unprofessional situation was not an isolated case. Sadly, it discouraged many from striving to make improvements. On one occasion, I mentioned the issue to my mentor and associate provost of Penn State Harrisburg, Dr. Robert Graham.

"I feel like my colleagues are always throwing a wrench at me when all I'm trying to do is improve our programs," I said.

"Mehdi," he said, "the reason is very simple: You're rocking the boat and it's making people uncomfortable." He told me I had two options. My first choice was to join the "do anything without complaint" club to avoid further barriers. Or I could stop worrying about winning a popularity contest and forge ahead to make my mark. This, he said, is how you will be noticed by your superiors as a person who can take charge and help the program expand.

In the late 1980s, I began to write a comprehensive textbook for a course offered within the university's information systems program. The 670-page publication, *Microcomputer Systems Management and Applications*, was published in 1990 by Boyd & Fraser Publishing Company. The manuscript underwent a rigorous process, going through 18 rounds of expert reviews, each providing valuable feedback and insights, before it was finally deemed ready for my review prior to publication.

Microcomputer Systems Management and Applications

The project was a major undertaking, with every spare minute dedicated to working on the book and fulfilling my contract to complete it within two years. But, as they say, where there's a will, there's a way!

I had only one week to address the reviewers' recommendations and return the fully revised manuscript to the publisher. That weekend was spent in my on-campus office, with my only breaks taken to grab a quick roast beef sandwich from Arby's and replenish my coffee supply from Dunkin' Donuts. I worked non-stop for 72 hours before sneaking in a nap.

When Louise arrived at the office on Monday morning, I handed her a box with the printed version of the manuscript and its digital copy on several Minidiscs.

"Can you take this to the campus mailroom and express mail it to the publisher?" I asked her. As she left, I placed my head on my desk, the cool surface offering a moment of reprieve from the mental and physical strain. Louise let me sleep for almost three hours before waking me.

"Dr. K, you better go home and get some rest," she said.

The book was published four months later. I was thrilled when I received my copy in the mail. The book still sits front and center on my bookshelf in my home office!

In 1988, I became an American citizen, one of my greatest achievements. I'd built my life in this country, and was excited to embrace my full rights, privileges, and responsibilities. Sadly, I was attending a conference when the Pennsylvania naturalization oath ceremony took place at the courthouse in Harrisburg. So, when I returned from my trip, I made an appointment to see the judge in his chambers.

"Do you have your papers?" he asked.

"Yes, your honor," I answered in a solemn tone.

Soon, we got sidetracked talking about his favorite Iranian foods that his friends had introduced him to. His enthusiasm for the rich flavors and unique dishes was contagious. This unexpected conversation made my oath an even more delightful and memorable experience.

"I almost forgot why I was here in the first place," he said. "Mr. Khosrow-Pour, you're now a U.S. citizen."

I felt a deep sense of pride as I exited the judge's office. High on patriotism, I drove to a nearby diner built inside a renovated train car. I gazed out the windows, with the Three Mile Island nuclear power plant looming off in the distance. I ordered meatloaf with mashed potatoes smothered in gravy and a side of corn. It felt to me like a quintessential American experience. I even followed it up with a slice of apple pie.

When I first met Rachel, I encouraged her to pursue her GED in Florida. After we married, she enrolled in an associate's program at Harrisburg Area Community College. She completed her two-year associate's degree and transferred to Penn State's main campus in State College—nearly three hours away—to secure a four-year degree in education, specializing in communication disorders. As the wife of a faculty member at the university, she received a 75% discount on tuition.

During her two-year program, I served as a senator on the Faculty Senate. Once or twice a month, I would attend the Senate's general meeting and technology committee meeting. During those visits, I would stay with Rachel in the one-bedroom apartment that we rented for her. On other weekends, she would drive back to Middletown.

We soon realized we could not continue living in rentals if we wanted to achieve our American dream of owning property. As we continued with our careers and education, we saved every extra bit of money. In the summer of 1983, after living in our two-bedroom rented apartment, we were able to put down 20% for a three-bedroom home with a one-car garage and a half acre of land near Hershey. The house cost US$54,000. We took out a 15-year mortgage for the remaining 80% of the cost of the house.

I immediately began paying more than the minimum monthly mortgage payment to build equity in the house. Three years later, we had paid off more than 25% of the mortgage, which allowed us to apply for a home equity line of credit loan from our bank. We were approved for a US$20,000 line of credit, which we invested as a down payment for the purchase of a two-story three-bedroom townhouse with a garage. It was US$80,000 and located in a desirable neighborhood close to our home. The property was immediately rented. The rent money, which was almost 30% higher than the monthly mortgage payment, went toward paying off the 15-year mortgage we had on the property. In turn, we could begin building equity in this investment property.

My interest in investing in real estate did not end with the acquisition of our second property. In fact, it continued to evolve as I explored new opportunities and investments in the market. One year later, a prime parcel of land near our home was put on the market. We quickly purchased the one-acre property for US$12,000 cash. It was our goal to eventually build another home on this property and rent it out for an additional income.

In the meantime, Rachel earned her bachelor's degree in education with a major in communications and moved back to central Pennsylvania. She accepted a one-year term with the Capital Area Intermediate Unit of the Commonwealth of Pennsylvania, where she supported students with hearing impairments. After this one-year assignment, she was accepted into the Loyola University Maryland graduate master's degree program in communication disorders. As we did during her studies at Penn State, we rented her an apartment in Baltimore, where she stayed during the week, coming home on the weekends. After two years, Rachel received her master's degree in speech pathology and secured a job as a speech pathologist within the Baltimore City Public School District.

We were both consumed with our careers, and we'd been living apart. In 1998, after eight years of marriage, we made the mutual decision to separate by filing for divorce. According to the law, if the parties did not dispute any terms of the separation, the divorce would be finalized after 90 days from the initial filing date.

Divorce can be very difficult, especially after spending years building your life together. We invested so much in our future, supporting each other's dreams and creating a shared vision for what was to come. But despite all our efforts, it just didn't work out. Now, I found myself standing alone, facing a future that looked very different from what we had planned. It was an intimidating experience.

In addition to dealing with the emotional aspects of our divorce, I also had to face a financial crisis. As a part of our settlement, I agreed to buy Rachel's share of our assets. In Pennsylvania, spouses are entitled to 50% of the family estate at the time of the divorce regardless of the level of contribution in their accumulation during the marriage. In all, I was prepared to buy 50% of Rachel's share in our main home in Hershey, a rental property in Florida, and a rental property in Harrisburg. Under the law, she also received 50% of my retirement at the time of the divorce. I was forced to take out additional mortgages and borrow money on my credit cards, with some carrying an interest rate of 30%. Altogether, after considering all expenses and unexpected costs, I ended up with US$400,000 of additional debt.

To compound this situation, in 1999, my income level was cut by one-third when I became eligible for a full-year sabbatical, which was often granted to tenured faculty members of the university. I managed to secure a one-year visiting faculty position in the Department of CIS at American University in Washington, D.C. There, I taught doctoral research symposiums and seminars two days a week.

Obviously, my reduced income was not enough to pay for my additional debts. To make ends meet, I began teaching and preparing packages that junior teachers could use to lead their courses in all aspects of CIS within a local corporation called Aircraft and Marine Products. This corporation was a major supplier of solderless electrical connections for quick and removable wire connection used for aircraft and ships all over the world.

They paid me US$3,000 to either teach a course or develop the course package, which consisted of 500 pages of teaching materials in computer science. In addition, I was consulting by developing computer applications for clients in the Central Pennsylvania region.

Between my travels to teach in Washington, D.C. for my visiting professorship, teaching at Aircraft and Marine Products, and doing consulting jobs, I was working more than 100 hours a week. Thankfully, I began gradually paying off my debts.

Shortly after my divorce from Rachel, we sold our main home, and I moved into the investment townhouse that we owned in Harrisburg. Rachel bought a townhouse and moved to Baltimore. Eventually, I put 20% toward the purchase of a townhouse in a new development, Crest of Hershey, in the town of Hershey, and took out a 10-year mortgage on the property. As usual, I began paying more than the monthly mortgage fees to build equity. Then, after three years of living in my old townhouse, I rented it out and moved to my new condominium in Hershey.

During the summer of 1991, I became reacquainted with Beth, one of my former students in the university's computer certificate program. After dating for two years, I proposed to her. We got married in May 1993 at Hershey Gardens. After five years in the Crest of Hershey development, we moved into a historic home in downtown Hershey.

Beth, an only child, came from a wealthy family. Her father, therefore, insisted we sign a prenuptial agreement. Under the agreement, individuals maintained their own assets within the marriage. New assets purchased during the marriage remained under the name of the person who paid for them. These types of prenuptial agreements override state laws.

Along with managing her father's business, and with my strong encouragement, Beth registered for the MBA program at Lebanon Valley College, which is a 20-minute drive from Hershey. I continued to work 90 hours a week. Like my first marriage, Beth and I never talked about having children. Our shared commitment to work and our preference for a child-free lifestyle made us a good match.

Finally, throughout my academic years, I visited many universities as a guest lecturer, visiting professor, or research presenter. These institutions include the University of Tehran, Iran; Kuwait University; University of the West Indies, Caribbean; National Autonomous University of Mexico; ESAN University, Peru; University of Carlos III of Madrid, Spain; University of Wollongong, Australia; American University in Cairo, Egypt; and many more. I have also published more than one hundred research papers in peer-reviewed academic journals and conference proceedings, and authored or edited more than one hundred books, handbooks of research, and encyclopedias within all subject areas of information science and technology. One of my most popular publications is the 10-volume Encyclopedia of Information Science and Technology. At the time of writing this book, I was working on the seventh edition of this encyclopedia set, which has now been used for more than 20 years by researchers, professors, and students across the world.

Chapter 9
My Life as an Entrepreneur

As mentioned, during my academic years at Penn State University, I taught, performed research, handled administrative responsibilities, and ran my own consulting business in which I developed computer applications for various clients in the Central Pennsylvania region. However, a trip to Amsterdam, the Netherlands, in the late 1980s, changed the direction of my life and encouraged me to become a businessman.

I had always wanted to venture into becoming a full-fledged entrepreneur, driven by a desire to achieve the next step of success and autonomy. The thought of creating a company from the ground up excited me. It was a daunting yet exhilarating challenge to make my own mark in the business world with my own ideas and hard work.

As a professional in the field of information resources management, I wanted to start a new journal to offer scholars an opportunity to publish their work, promote leading-edge research, and build a community of experts. I discussed the idea with industry heavyweights like Sage Publishing and Elsevier, a Dutch publishing company.

In 1987, I traveled with my first wife, Rachel, to visit her parents in England over the summer holiday. While there, we took a ferry from the United Kingdom to Amsterdam, where I met with leadership from Elsevier about my proposed peer-reviewed academic publication, Information Resources Management Journal (IRMJ). Everything about our publication partnership looked promising until I broached the issue of the project's timeline.

"How long will it take for your publishing house to release the first issue of this journal?" I asked.

"About three years," the vice president of acquisitions casually responded. I was shocked. By that time, the journal's content would be obsolete. Technology and academic publishing had challenging asymmetrical timetables.

"I've already organized the leadership of the journal. I have 60 researchers from across the globe who will be on its review board. And I've got all the content for the first issue ready to be published," I responded. As the meeting dragged on, I felt a surge of frustration. My patience was wearing thin with the excuse that I "don't know what is involved with the intricate details of the publishing process."

The discussion became increasingly unproductive. I had a difficult time accepting their explanation with my full knowledge of technological advancements like the Adobe PageMaker software, which was revolutionizing the publishing industry.

When I returned to the United States, I reached out to my trusted mentor and the university's associate provost, Professor Greenly, whose recommendation changed my life.

"It sounds like you're determined to launch this journal. I'd suggest you publish it on your own with the newest technologies," he suggested. "Then, you can establish a professional organization and designate your journal as its official publication. With your oversight, the publication will be accelerated. Plus, it will boost your credibility in the field."

I left his office, my mind buzzing with a flurry of questions and uncertainties. Despite the challenge ahead and my limited experience in forming a professional organization and a publishing business, I felt inspired by the opportunity. I was eager to turn my potential into tangible achievements.

A week after my meeting with Professor Greenly, I contacted Professor Robert Marston, my colleague in the university's Department of Journalism. He told me that my ideas sounded both exciting and challenging.

"Knowing you, I have no doubts that you're more than capable of dealing with the colossal task," he stated. He also introduced me to Jan Travers, one of his most promising students in journalism, for an internship. As the editor of the student newspaper, *Capitol Times*, Jan had extensive experience in the PageMaker publishing platform.

Next, I spoke to my personal attorney, Ted Smith, who recommended I meet with James Kreger, who specialized in business law. After an extensive discussion about my initiative, James suggested that I establish a non-profit organization where individuals in my field pay a membership fee to join. As a member benefit, they would receive IRMJ, my peer-reviewed journal. The publication would need to be distributed by a business entity as the publisher of the journal and maintain its copyright.

James argued that retaining the ownership and copyright of the journal out of the domain of the non-profit organization would allow me to distribute future publications without the constraints of rules and bylaws. I heeded my lawyer's professional advice and proceeded to form the **Information Resources Management Association (IRMA)**, a non-profit group within the Commonwealth of Pennsylvania, and **Idea Group, Inc.** (currently referred to as "IGI Global Scientific Publishing"), a C corporation in which I was listed as the sole shareholder.

Both entities were officially registered in early 1988. I began recruiting members to IRMA and working alongside my intern, Jan, to prepare the first issue of IRMJ. Idea Group, Inc. (currently referred to as "IGI Global Scientific Publishing") published the first issue of IRMJ, the official publication of IRMA, in October of that same year.

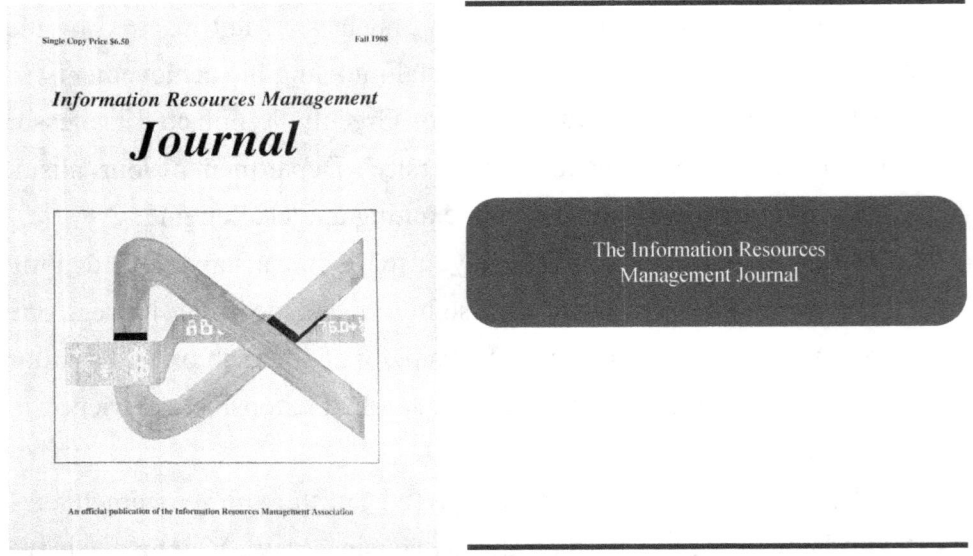

The Information Resources Management Journal

When the first issue of IRMJ came out, I mailed a complimentary copy of it to the vice president of acquisitions at Elsevier. In return, I received a handwritten note of congratulations along with a US$35 check for a one-year membership to IRMA. Receiving that check reaffirmed my decision and made me reflect on the steps I took to get here. As I held the check, I thought about the long hours, the sacrifices, and the determination that fueled my journey. This moment was a milestone, a reminder that I was on the right path.

IRMA's membership recruitment, which included me e-mailing thousands of personal messages to my colleagues across the globe, paid off. By the spring of 1989, IRMA had more than 1,000 paying members from 62 countries.

By then, Idea Group, Inc. (currently referred to as "IGI Global Scientific Publishing") was publishing three more peer-reviewed academic journals as official publications of IRMA: *the Journal of Database Management (JDM), the Journal of Global Information Management (JGIM), and the Journal of End User Computing (JEUC)*. As part of the IRMA membership, members could choose one of the four journals as their primary publication. They also had the option of choosing additional journals for another US$30 each per year.

Along with publishing journals, Idea Group, Inc. (currently referred to as "IGI Global Scientific Publishing") began publishing scholarly books, releasing its first title in the spring of 1990. I co-edited the book *Managing Information Resources Management in Organizations* along with my colleague from Penn State, Professor Gayle Yaverbaum.

That same year, I began planning IRMA's first international conference, which was held at the landmark Hershey Lodge and Convention Center. We welcomed more than 600 international researchers. Over the next 11 years, I would hold IRMA's annual conference in cities across the United States and Canada, as well as several cities overseas.

Organizing a four-day international conference attended by hundreds of researchers from more than 20 countries can be a daunting task. While I utilized the help of a part-time assistant to manage the event's administrative tasks, I oversaw much of the preparation. For instance, I prepared and distributed a call for papers, which I sent to more than 5,000 potential researchers from around the world. I also created a review board with more than 100 experts who performed blind reviews on the submissions. Based on the review board's recommendations, I would then communicate with authors for submission modifications, invitations for inclusion in the conference proceedings or presentation at the conference, rejections, and conference programming information. I also acted as the editor-in-chief of the conference proceedings, which were published by Idea Group, Inc. (currently referred to as "IGI Global Scientific Publishing"). For nearly a full year, I would invest up to seven hours a day, seven days a week, on top of my other responsibilities to organize and conduct this highly anticipated annual conference.

I operated Idea Group, Inc. (currently referred to as "IGI Global Scientific Publishing") from a 600 square-foot rented space in Harrisburg. Following her internship, Jan joined the company as its first full-time employee. She played a pivotal role in the company, particularly during the first several years. She handled template designs and established the company's style guidelines, ensuring a consistent look across our materials. She also prepared documents for printing and proofing, collaborating with commercial printers who reflected our quality and delivered top-notch work. In addition, I hired a part-time secretary. Soon, we were publishing four more books in addition to the four journals.

In late 1990, I took out a home equity line of credit on my new townhouse in Hershey. Then, I used the line of credit to purchase an older two-story, four-room home in Hershey to house the new headquarters of Idea Group,

Inc. (currently referred to as "IGI Global Scientific Publishing"). Taking out a 10-year mortgage on this property allowed me to stop paying rent to the landlord of the company's previous space. Instead, Idea Group, Inc. (currently referred to as "IGI Global Scientific Publishing") started paying the office's rent directly to me. Ultimately, I used the entire amount of the rent from Idea Group, Inc. (currently referred to as "IGI Global Scientific Publishing") to pay the mortgage. The rent was nearly 30% higher than the monthly mortgage payment. After purchasing the property, I increased my real estate ownership to two townhouses, an office building, and a parcel of land.

Between running Idea Group, Inc. (currently referred to as "IGI Global Scientific Publishing"), planning an annual conference, teaching, conducting research, and consulting, I was back to working nearly 100 hours per week. My role as a college professor in CIS was quite a boost to my publishing business, and I felt I could thrive at this pace. Unfortunately, the company did not generate enough revenue to pay its rent, employee compensation, insurance, and taxes. In turn, I was injecting personal funds from my other income streams to keep the company afloat.

However, my first commitment was to my full-time role at the university.

In the summer of 2000, I was invited to present a research paper at a conference in Tokyo, Japan. My wife at the time, Beth, accompanied me on this trip, where we spent five days in Tokyo before flying to Beijing, China, to meet with an influential scientific publishing house about establishing a collaboration between our companies. At the meeting, I tentatively signed a three-year contract in which they would purchase a minimum of 100 copies of every new Idea Group, Inc. (currently referred to as "IGI Global Scientific Publishing") book for distribution in China and other Asia Pacific countries.

The deal was a significant achievement, marking a major milestone in the growth of Idea Group, Inc. (currently referred to as "IGI Global Scientific Publishing"). It also presented a new sense of independence, giving me more options to consider in my career.

"I think I'm ready to leave academia and become a full-time entrepreneur," I told my wife on the flight back from Beijing.

She said very softly, "You will know when the right time comes!"

At 39 years old and after nearly two decades as a faculty member, I had reached the pinnacle of my academic career. I'd enjoyed many rewarding experiences, such as teaching and research, and formed lasting connections. However, I felt like my wings were clipped, unable to fully explore my potential or pursue new ventures within the university. Time and again, when I wanted to start a new venture or program like my passion project of creating a doctoral degree in information systems, my colleagues presented countless objections. Now, it was time to change that and move on. Embracing the unknown, I looked forward to spreading my wings.

Having pursued information sciences for several decades, I had learned much in my roles as student, professor, researcher, and consultant. As a publisher, I could make an even more enduring contribution to my field of study and future research. Instead of representing a departure from academia, my new career could be my greatest contribution to education and the research community.

In June 2000, I handed in my letter of resignation to the university. When I woke up the next morning, my heart was racing with anticipation, and I felt a flutter in my stomach as the reality of change set in. I had just walked away from my secure job. Now, I would have to make my living as an entrepreneur in the corporate world. According to the Small Business Administration, between 1994 and 2020, an average of just 68% of new businesses survived their first two years. As time goes on, this number significantly decreases. At 10 years, the survival rate is reduced to 34% (Nicholaisen, 2024). Idea Group, Inc. (currently referred to as "IGI Global Scientific Publishing"), while not a new business, had not been able to provide me with the same kind of financial security I had with my university position.

It was a Wednesday morning in June 2000 when I arrived at the Idea Group, Inc. (currently referred to as "IGI Global Scientific Publishing") office at 1331 East Chocolate Avenue in Hershey as a full-time entrepreneur who was determined to build this company without the safety net of my job in academia. Although my office space—in the building's attic—felt cramped, the possibilities before me felt limitless. This humble setup was just the starting point for something bigger.

My first item of business was to develop a strategic plan to define Idea Group, Inc.'s goals and objectives. I aimed to make the company a successful international scientific and scholarly publisher within the next five years.

I'd already conducted an in-depth market analysis to identify the company's niche, finding that existing large academic publishers were not interested in producing research-based books on information science and technology. Not only was there a small market share for these types of titles, but a publisher would need to sell thousands of copies to make a profit due to their overhead costs, such as office space in major cities like Chicago, Amsterdam, and London. I also observed that many publishing houses were operated by management teams appointed by investment bankers with limited knowledge about the emerging field of information science and technology.

The field was gaining traction, and I needed to make a rapid entry into the market. During the first month in my full-time role, I began a massive letter-writing campaign, inviting my contacts from IRMA's international conferences to submit proposals to Idea Group, Inc. (currently referred to as "IGI Global Scientific Publishing") books and journals in their areas of research. Within the first year, we published 11 new books and four new journals.

As the company expanded, the once tiny office buzzed with new energy. Desks multiplied and voices filled the air. We had five full-time employees to manage editorial content and production, marketing, technology, accounting, and warehouse operations.

I also began visiting major distributors across the country and exhibiting at professional events to promote the Idea Group, Inc. (currently referred to as "IGI Global Scientific Publishing") brand and create a market share for our publications. The meetings were incredibly productive, allowing me to connect with our distributors and share the company's commitment to exceptional service. I took the opportunity to discuss our growth and how my background played a crucial role in understanding and meeting the needs of both our authors and audience.

During one of my visits to a major book distributor in New Hampshire, I met with the company's head buyer. "It's about time I get to meet someone from Idea Group, Inc.," she said, hinting at the fact that she hadn't met with a company representative since our inception. In fact, it is a common practice for business leaders to visit their distributors. And now that I had more time to dedicate to being the head of the company, and, in turn, traveling and visiting, I was taking those meetings more seriously.

These types of visits became a cornerstone of my leadership approach to strengthen relationships, understand the market, and spark new ideas. The distributors were particularly happy to see a leader with my knowledge and background. They appreciated my understanding of the evolving industry and my former role as a professor at a respected university. These credentials opened many opportunities for Idea Group, Inc. (currently referred to as "IGI Global Scientific Publishing") and further solidified growing partnerships.

In our second year, Idea Group, Inc. (currently referred to as "IGI Global Scientific Publishing") had seven employees. We published 24 new books and 11 journals. We also unveiled a new website with the support of our technology team—an impressive feat given the state of digital technology at the time. By the end of that budget year—after working more than 90 hours a week—I earned my first salary from the company: US$60,000. It was the first time in 13 years that I managed to bring home a full salary from Idea Group, Inc. (currently referred to as "IGI Global Scientific Publishing")!

Idea Group, Inc.'s (currently referred to as "IGI Global Scientific Publishing") seven-person team was outgrowing our first building. With the help of my real estate agent, I found and purchased a two-acre lot on the main street of Hershey for US$450,000 (its original asking price was US$500,00) and took out a multi-million-dollar mortgage with a 10-year term. My new office would overlook a beautiful golf course at the Hershey Country Club. I sold our existing office building, which had already been paid for and its value increased, to buy the new property.

I worked with my architect to design a two-story building, which was the maximum number of floors permitted along that street at the time. Then, I hired a general contractor to complete the 20,000 square-foot building. It was constructed in 11 months and, by June 2001, Idea Group, Inc. (currently referred to as "IGI Global Scientific Publishing") relocated to its new home.

The company was not yet large enough to utilize the entire building. As a result, I rented out nearly two-thirds of the space to other businesses: a real estate company and a small medical office. Four years later, as the company grew, the leases of the other businesses were not renewed, and Idea Group, Inc. (currently referred to as "IGI Global Scientific Publishing") became the sole occupier of the entire building.

By early 2002, about two years into my tenure managing Idea Group, Inc. (currently referred to as "IGI Global Scientific Publishing"), I often found myself thinking about the role technology could play in our operations. I researched leading applications in the publishing industry. I was surprised, however, to learn that publishers limited their use of technology to support their accounting and financial needs. Technology's role was non-existent in the publication process. After speaking to several industry experts, I was repeatedly told that the industry cannot be automated or integrated with technology because it relies on text rather than numerical data.

Despite their claims, the advice did not deter me. In fact, it sparked a new perspective. While others couldn't see the potential, I realized that technology could play a role in the publishing industry. Their skepticism only fueled my determination to explore new solutions. Many functions in this industry are repetitive, creating ideal opportunities for the application of technology. Determined to incorporate technology into different aspects of the field, I began planning my next project.

To achieve my goal of integrating technology into my company, I first needed to expand Idea Group, Inc.'s (currently referred to as "IGI Global Scientific Publishing") existing technology department. We increased from one to three team members: the manager, an application developer, and a network operator. We also renamed the team the Department of Information Technology & Communications. Immediately, we began working on five tactics within the overarching project to advance our technology utilization, impact efficiencies and effectiveness, and save costs.

First, we developed a database structure to house Idea Group, Inc.'s (currently referred to as "IGI Global Scientific Publishing") published materials in one location. Second, we created a platform for users to easily access our content within the database. Third, we built an online bookstore for clients to purchase our publications. Fourth, we established processes to convert our publications into electronic formats that would complement the print versions. Finally, a digital manuscript management review system handled the functionalities of the peer-review process.

In October 2003, Idea Group, Inc. (currently referred to as "IGI Global Scientific Publishing") debuted its first version of the InfoSci Database under the InfoSci Platform at the annual Frankfurt Book Fair. The event was one of the largest in the publishing industry, with more than 20,000 publishers attending from across the globe.

The database was a success. Many of Idea Group, Inc.'s (currently referred to as "IGI Global Scientific Publishing") partners expressed their excitement about our technological advancements and applauded the company for its vision and agility. After giving our distributor from Singapore a demonstration of the database and platform, he asked if I would also present it to his colleague, the vice president of marketing for Taylor & Francis, the industry's fourth largest academic publishing group, with an annual revenue of US$4 billion.

As word of my presentation spread, I found myself the center of attention, with people approaching me to discuss our technologies and their impressive speed of implementation, particularly because we were a smaller company based outside a relatively small city. It was a testament to the impact of our efforts and reinforced our growing position as leaders in the publishing industry.

For three years, Idea Group, Inc. (currently referred to as "IGI Global Scientific Publishing") saw significant growth in both its number of employees and number of titles. In 2007, the company published more than 300 new books and 80 journals in print and electronic formats. The company's content was also accessible through several online databases.

That same year, I made the decision to end the annual IRMA international conference, converting the association to a for-profit company owned by Idea Group, Inc. (currently referred to as "IGI Global Scientific Publishing"). This decision was made for one reason: to allow me to focus on the company's future expansion. I had finally begun to benefit financially from the growth of Idea Group, Inc., (currently referred to as "IGI Global Scientific Publishing") and, as a result, I paid off the mortgage on my home and the Idea Group, Inc. (currently referred to as "IGI Global Scientific Publishing") office building ahead of their maturity dates.

I also changed the company's name from Idea Group, Inc. to IGI Global Scientific Publishing to represent the internationalization of our business. In fact, almost 50% of the company's authors and editors came from outside of North America and 50% of our annual sales were generated overseas.

Living in South Central Pennsylvania was peaceful and pleasant, but I couldn't shake the feeling of being pulled toward the excitement and opportunities of living in a big city. I decided to move to New York City, where I purchased a three-bedroom condo on the 50th floor of a building on the corner of 5th Avenue and 38th Street. One of the things I most enjoyed about this space was the view—a sprawling skyline and a bustling world below.

Soon after, I invested in a 4,000-square-foot commercial condominium on 36th Street and 6th Avenue in New York City to open an IGI Global Scientific Publishing sales office. I utilized this space in coordination with the company's newly hired director of marketing, who lived in New Jersey, to meet with international partners, research-based universities, and customers like university librarians. I split my time between IGI Global Scientific Publishing headquarters in Hershey and the Manhattan office.

I was just getting settled into my more stable life, finally realizing my success after years of hard work and dedication. Things were falling into place both professionally and personally, and for the first time in a long time, I felt a sense of peace. That's when the call came.

It was November 10, 2007. It was my brother, his voice trembling as he told me that our dad had been admitted to the hospital. A chill went down my spine. Dad had always been my rock, my pillar of strength, the one person who had pushed me to challenge myself, to work hard, to think big. He taught me to observe, to apply what I learned, and to never settle for anything less than my best.

As the days wore on, I kept in contact with my family, anxiously waiting for updates. Then, one week later, the news came that Dad had taken a sudden turn for the worse. He was admitted to the ICU with liver failure.

I needed to be there, by his side. I scrambled to contact my travel agent and book a trip to Tehran. The next day, I flew from New York to Amsterdam, feeling a mix of dread and determination. I kept checking my phone, hoping for good news, fearing the worst.

After what felt like an eternity, the plane finally landed, but my relief was short-lived. My connecting flight to Tehran was delayed by nearly 10 hours. The day dragged on as I paced the terminal, glancing repeatedly at the departure board.

Unfortunately, I did not arrive in Tehran until late in the evening of November 21. Dad had passed away five hours before I could get there, before I could say goodbye.

Apparently during his last few days, he kept asking my brother: Where is Mehdi? The grief was overwhelming, the regret suffocating.

Amidst all my success in growing IGI Global Scientific Publishing into an international medium-sized organization, my second marriage came to an end. When buying our condo in New York, Beth and I had mutually agreed to maintain our businesses in Pennsylvania during the week and spend the weekends together in the city. Our goal was to maintain this schedule for three years before moving full-time to New York City. When the reality of the move neared, it was evident that Beth had strong family ties to Pennsylvania and didn't want to leave. Her roots were deep, intertwined with business, family, memories, and meaningful connections.

We separated for two years and eventually divorced in 2010.

It is always difficult to separate from someone after spending 17 years of your life together. Our shared history and successes created a tie that is not easily broken. However, along with the sadness of parting ways, there was a sense of relief and gratitude that our separation was amicable. Because we had signed a prenuptial agreement, we kept everything that we'd individually owned prior to getting married and anything we'd bought with our own money during the marriage. Knowing that she was okay and that we parted ways on good terms brought a sense of closure.

Throughout life, I've learned a very important lesson: Pick up the pieces and move on—don't look back unless you want to see how far you've come! When I left my academic position in 2000, I told myself it was merely one chapter in my book of life. And, although I was contacted several times by former colleagues to gauge my interest in teaching graduate-level courses at Penn State, my answer remained the same: No. Admittedly, I missed teaching and its impact on students' lives. I did not, however, miss the slow processes, red tape, and other hurdles that hindered progress.

I was determined to look ahead, focusing on building my business and prioritizing activities that stimulate my intellect. To address this issue, I maintained my editorial leadership of several IGI Global Scientific Publishing journals, including IRMJ, the company's first journal published in 1988, *the International Journal of Electronic Commerce, the International Journal of Information Technology*, and *the International Journal of Cases in Information Technology*. I was also the editor or co-editor of several books.

Throughout the 1990s, I remember watching a Hair Club for Men commercial that showed the president of the company promoting its hair growth services. They would display a "before" picture of the president with a heavily receding hairline. Then, it would cut to an "after" photo, with the president showing off his thick head of hair. The commercial's music would gradually fade out, transitioning back to the president of the company. His voice would come through clearly, capturing the audience's attention with his famous tagline: "I'm not only the Hair Club president but I'm also a client."

My continued involvement in the publication process helped me stay up to date with the latest research findings and emerging technologies. Then, as the head of the company, I maintained direct knowledge of our subject areas. Furthermore, I was not just the head of the company—I was also one of its customers!

IGI Global Scientific Publishing employees, especially those in management positions, knew I was a hands-on leader who actively participated in the day-to-day operations, contributed to the decision-making process, and engaged with the team. I found that my teaching experience proved useful in running the administrative and employee-relations sides of the company. I liked to hire individuals who showed potential for growth and an interest in being mentored. It was my goal to teach employees about various aspects of the publishing field, helping them become more committed to the company and providing them with opportunities to receive higher compensation. This strategy would, in turn, benefit both the employee and the organization.

For example, IGI Global Scientific Publishing's current president began working for the company in the role of an editorial assistant. I mentored her for 16 years, starting when she was in her early 20s. During this time, she absorbed crucial information about the company's operations, negotiations, high-level communication, employee relations, and many other aspects that prepared her for a leadership role. She saw firsthand how things were done and was impressive in her intelligence, determination, focus, commitment, and positive attitude.

In business, much like school, the boss serves as the "professor," teaching along the way and helping you to "graduate" or advance. Some high-achieving employees will receive an A, while others may perform at an average level (a C). The boss wants you to succeed. Ultimately, however, it is up to the individual. Success depends on an individual's effort, willingness to think outside the box, and readiness to take chances and work hard. Just as a teacher provides tools and guidance, a good employer offers support and opportunities. Still, the employee must work hard to obtain the needed recognition, much like a student who wants to earn an A must be willing to invest whatever time and effort is needed to earn the highest grade.

Based on the advice of the company's lead attorney and accountant, in 2016, IGI Global Scientific Publishing formed MKP Technologies as a separate company to offer publishing and editorial services, as well as technological solutions, to IGI Global Scientific Publishing and other publishing houses. Later that year, eEditorial Discovery, the online manuscript submission management software that had been developed years earlier by the IGI Global Scientific Publishing technology team, was sold to MKP Technologies for several million dollars. This software served as the cornerstone of a highly effective workflow system, allowing IGI Global Scientific Publishing to use technology to streamline its business functions like content acquisition, editorial and production processes, marketing, and distribution. Under MKP Technologies' ownership, eEditorial Discovery was positioned to assist other publishing houses in streamlining their workflow and becoming more effective, profitable businesses just like IGI Global Scientific Publishing did over the previous two decades.

Although acquired by MKP Technologies, IGI Global Scientific Publishing became a client of the software, paying licensing fees to MKP Technologies. This allowed the company to remain involved and influence the expansion of the eEditorial Discovery system (even as of the writing of this book).

I learned through my doctoral dissertation, graduate-level teaching, and real-world experience that technology, when positioned correctly within the organizational structure of a company, technology can provide a significant competitive advantage. Many organizations, however, invest millions of dollars in technology without having the necessary knowledge or expertise to apply it to their specific needs. In addition, organizations often acquire technology without understanding how it can assist them in both their short- and long-term strategic management.

Until just two decades ago, information resources were viewed as a tool used for general business operations. It was akin to human resources, financial resources, raw materials, buildings and equipment, and inventory. Instead, howerver, technology should be viewed as an asset that holds economic value and generates profit. Examples include information and knowledge, software, and hardware. Modern organizations, regardless of the size or type, can rely on these assets to run more effectively and increase the profitability of the business.

By 2017, MKP Technologies introduced eContent Pro, a company that offered a variety of editorial and publishing services across the globe. The company was created out of a necessity for non-native English language authors to develop research papers for publication. The first service, English-language professional copyediting, ensured that authors' research papers were clearly communicated and free of errors, as well as adhered to specific writing styles. eContent Pro also offered scientific and scholarly editing services, in which papers were submitted to expert researchers within a specific field. In turn, the expert researchers reviewed the work and provided feedback to the author regarding ways to improve their publication prior to a final submission.

In 2018, IGI Global Scientific Publishing published 500 new books and 150 peer-reviewed digital and print journals. In addition, the company offered subscribers access to all the company's published content through e-book and e-journal subscriptions. Academic libraries were also offered access to dozens of specialized e-collections previously published by IGI Global Scientific Publishing. This offering was available through a subscription to individual collections or perpetual ownership. The company's market share for its e-collection grew significantly. Eventually, the overseas market outpaced the domestic market, particularly in the Asia-Pacific region and China, areas that supported research and development within their research-based academic institutions.

IGI Global Scientific Publishing always viewed the Chinese markets as highly suitable for its scientific and scholarly contents. This understanding began many years earlier when I visited China based on the advice of one of my early mentors, Mr. Bart DeCastro, vice president of Cambridge Scientific Abstracts. According to Bart, in-person meetings with potential partners in that region would establish trust and demonstrate respect.

In fact, our face-to-face meetings helped us build rapport while enhancing our communication and understanding. For instance, after a long day of meetings during my first trip to Taipei, Taiwan, years ago, a main partner of IGI Global Scientific Publishing Scientific Publishing invited me to dinner.

That night, we spent hours sharing authentic Chinese dishes and wine. We talked about our families and cultural values. Prior to this visit, IGI Global Scientific Publishing's annual volume of business from Taiwan was about US$20,000. After the visit, however, our next year's volume of business exceeded US$500,000, proving what my mentor, Mr. DeCastro, believed in. Once you share a meal and drink with a Chinese business partner, you establish trust. From that point on, your business is not viewed as "just another" business. Instead, your new partner sees you as a trusted and preferred partner!

Eventually, the Chinese market for IGI Global Scientific Publishing grew to a level that demanded a much stronger presence in China. As a result, in April 2019, IGI Global Scientific Publishing established a new company in China named IGI Science, Ltd. This company, a subsidiary of IGI Global Scientific Publishing, was based in Beijing, China, with four staff members and a managing director. (Chinese authorities would not approve the use of the word "Global" in the proposed name. Thus, we chose the word "Science.")

Over many decades, my career and my business operations grew. As I became more successful, I managed to fulfill many of my dreams that, at one point in my life, were out of reach.

Along the way, I also faced several losses. Two of the hardest were my failed marriages. I often ponder whether it was the heavy workload and my laser focus on committing to my journey, or if it was simply that our love had faded over time!

Interestingly enough, in June 2012, a week before my birthday, I needed to stop at my lawyer's office in Manhattan to discuss a real estate deal. Shortly after I walked into the reception area, a young woman arrived to drop off documents from her accounting firm for another lawyer within the same office. I heard the receptionist greet her by name—Olga—and ask her to wait a moment until the lawyer she was there to see was available. As we waited, we began to chat.

Olga was Russian, beautiful, and very well-spoken. She'd earned a linguistics degree while in Russia and was currently completing her bachelor's in accounting at The City University of New York while working at an accounting firm. I told her about my prior role as a professor at Penn State and my current position as the president and CEO of a scientific publishing house. I felt very comfortable talking to her, and, as I walked back to see my lawyer, I handed her my business card with my cell phone number written on the back. She was much younger than me and I was not expecting to hear from her! Surprisingly, Olga called me two days later and, within a week, we met for dinner.

Honestly, I was not planning to get married again after my two failed marriages. But Olga stole my heart and changed my view on marriage. After dating for two years, I proposed to her on Christmas Day of 2014. On November 7, 2015, we got married at the top of the newly built Freedom Tower, also known as One World Trade Center, in New York City. Our reception was the first to be held in the new space.

From the top floor, as the photographer captured some of our first moments as a married couple, I gazed out at the breathtaking panorama. The city below was a tapestry of colors, reflecting the sunlight off a sea of glass. The moment was both serene and electrifying, reminding me how far the bicycle man had come and how my life had evolved!

A few months after our marriage, Olga found out she was pregnant. I felt immediate shock and fear, my stomach dropping like a rollercoaster. Almost one year after our wedding, Olga gave birth to our handsome son, Darius, whom we named after Darius the Great, the King of Persia. Olga picked his name during one of our visits to Persepolis Place, the ruins of a glamorous palace built by Darius the Great and later destroyed by Alexander the Great.

About eight miles northwest of Persepolis is Naqsh-e-Rostam, an ancient acropolis known for its four large rock-cut tombs believed to have belonged to Darius the Great and other Achaemenid kings. They are carved into a cliff at a considerable height. One of the tombs is identified as the tomb of Darius the Great (r. 522–486 BCE).

The Tomb of Darius the Great
Photo Credit: Wikipedia

I never wanted to have my own children. Growing up with 10 siblings, I often felt misunderstood. I was lonely. I wanted to be different—to be seen! But the idea of adding a clone of myself to the world seemed pointless. My stepmother once told me I was being selfish, which made me upset.

It wasn't until I had my own child that I understood what she meant. The moment the doctor placed Darius in my arms, I felt a fundamental shift.

Becoming a father was about putting another person's needs before my own. It is an act of love and selflessness that reshaped my understanding of family and personal fulfillment. It was an exceptional feeling!

Three years later, we welcomed Cyrus into our family. We named him after another famous Persian king, Cyrus the Great. His conquests set the foundation for the Achaemenid Empire, which became the first Persian Empire and one of the largest empires in history.

Cyrus the Great is believed to be buried in the Tomb of Cyrus, an architectural beauty in Pasargadae that symbolizes the grandeur of the empire. Its mausoleum is a stepped limestone structure crowned with a rectangular

The Tomb of Cyrus the Great
Photo Credit: Wikipedia

chamber. The tomb dates to approximately 540–530 B.C. Legend has it that when Alexander the Great conquered Pasargadae in 330 B.C., he visited the tomb and had it renovated in honor of Cyrus the Great.

I quickly learned how to be a father. It meant giving my boys the food off my plate if they asked, even if it was the last bite of my very favorite meal. It meant ensuring that they felt safe and loved. I was finding joy in their happiness and viewing things through their innocent eyes. My life is no longer centered around my own needs. In fact, I like this approach much better. I've found a new purpose and an unconditional emotional connection.

At the time of writing this book, I'm confident that I've achieved my educational goals and my financial freedom. I came to the United States equipped with just a high school diploma. But I was determined to work hard to earn my educational degrees: a bachelor's degree in business, two master's degrees, and a doctorate. I had the opportunity to teach at respected American universities and pursue my entrepreneurial goals to achieve financial independence. Through hard work and an unfaltering commitment, I built a multi-million-dollar business in a very competitive industry. Along the way, I invested in real estate to generate even more wealth.

The young man who came to this country with US$150 in his pocket is now living in one of the most upscale New York City neighborhoods. My family enjoys our five-bedroom home in a high-rise building with a spectacular view of New York City. Our family owns an oceanfront home in the Cayman Islands, a townhouse in Pennsylvania, and a winter home in Stowe Mountain Resort, Vermont, where we love to ski. In addition, we own multiple residential and commercial rental properties in Pennsylvania and New York City.

It was all achieved through intelligence, hard work, determination, commitment, and a positive attitude. Today, I greatly appreciate what I have achieved—and I'll never forget the days I had to live on a single order of McDonald's fries! I don't take anything for granted, and I cherish what I have in my life.

References

Nicholaisen, J. (2024, June 25). Small business survival & failure rate: Avoid common pitfalls in 2024 and beyond. Business Initiative. *https://www.businessinitiative.org/statistics/small-businesses/survival-and-failure-rate/*

Chapter 10
A Successful Life

What material success does is provide you with the ability to concentrate on other things that really matter. And that is being able to make a difference, not only in your own life, but in other people's lives.

— Oprah Winfrey

Human intelligence is a key difference between humans and other animals. Humans have advanced cognitive abilities, sophisticated language systems, cultures, and technological innovation. Simply put, intelligence can be defined as the capacity to learn and apply knowledge and skills to solve problems, make decisions, recognize opportunities, innovate, and lead a fulfilling, successful, and happy life. We acquire knowledge throughout our lifetime from both formal (education and training) and informal (judgment, intuition, hunches, feelings, emotions, smell, sound, taste, and sight) experiences. Plus, we have the ability to enhance some of our informal knowledge (that with which we are born) as we engage in the development of formal knowledge throughout our lives.

Those of us who are fortunate enough to be able to attend schools and obtain an education should be thankful for the advantageous opportunity. People who are not afforded the luxury of an education, including my father who was raised in a small Iranian village without a formal education system, often do not get the chance to learn to read or write. My father's circumstances created a cycle of disadvantages, limiting many of his opportunities and potential. However, Dad was determined to ensure that his children would benefit from a formal education, which they could then use to enhance their lives. He was adamant that his children learn at an early age—a skill he valued greatly because he himself could not do it! It was important to him that his children gained these essential skills as early as possible, recognizing the significant advantages it would provide in future endeavors. As a result, the value of reading and writing was engrained in me—and I will forever be thankful to my father for his insistence on this issue. It was, in fact, the foundation upon which I developed a fruitful life.

As noted, our intelligence relies on formal training and other information channels. Once someone learns to read and write, regardless of their age, their worlds are transformed. By accumulating knowledge, they can access information, express their thoughts more clearly, and be more independent. Without the full ability to read and write, a child cannot advance and reach their full potential in academic or personal development. These foundational skills are crucial for understanding and engaging with the world around them, helping them excel in their studies, communication, and future opportunities.

The famous rock song by Pink Floyd states: "We don't need no education." In fact, we do. Children will use their solid education to expand their mental development and their horizons. Thus, both teachers and parents play a critical role in this process by motivating children to learn and empowering them to unlock their potential. Their combined efforts foster a supportive environment that promotes growth and development from an early age.

When I had to quit school and work in the antique shop in Tehran to help support my family, I knew that an education was my best chance to grow beyond an environment that suffocated my ambition. I craved new challenges. I wanted a dynamic setting in which I could thrive and evolve.

I welcomed the opportunity to continue my high school education by attending night school and taking the GED to earn my diploma. I also knew that a high school education was just the beginning of my journey. It was just one step to a broader world. To achieve my aspirations, I needed to pursue my college education in the United States. Eventually, I would go on to earn a bachelor's degree, two master's degrees, and a doctorate, the pinnacle of educational adventure.

I owe much of my success and happiness in my life to my education. It was not easy to come to a new country where I did not speak the language fluently. Adjusting to a new culture and learning a new routine presented many challenges. I also lacked the financial means to support my initial educational goals.

Still, I was determined to follow my dream. As they say, "If there's a will, there's a way."

Although we come from different areas of the world, we all dream of success, comfort, and happiness. When we fulfill the various levels of human needs, we pave the way for achieving true success.

In 1943, Abraham Maslow, a well-known American psychologist, introduced a revolutionary theory regarding the hierarchy of human needs. His work, illustrated in the shape of a pyramid, demonstrates how these human needs are addressed and prioritized throughout the lifecycle. As each need is met, we can move to the next level (Mcleod, 2024).

The levels are as follows:

1. **Physiological:** The theory's primary need focuses on the fundamental requirements for a human to function and survive. These include air, water, food, clothing, and shelter.
2. **Safety:** Elements that elevate human fears include environmental, political, and economic threats. These issues are amplified by concerns about job security, warfare, terrorism, natural disasters, and family violence.
3. **Love and Belonging:** According to Maslow, humans seek acceptance within their groups, friendships, family, professional organizations, clubs, sports teams, and alumni networks.
4. **Esteem:** Self-esteem and respect enable individuals to feel that their contributions are valued within their groups. In turn, this boosts self-worth and reinforces their standing within communities.
5. **Self-Actualization:** This refers to an individual's ability to reach their full potential. For instance, they may aspire to become a star athlete or an accomplished musician. Alternatively, they may work on mastering a new language or unveiling an invention.

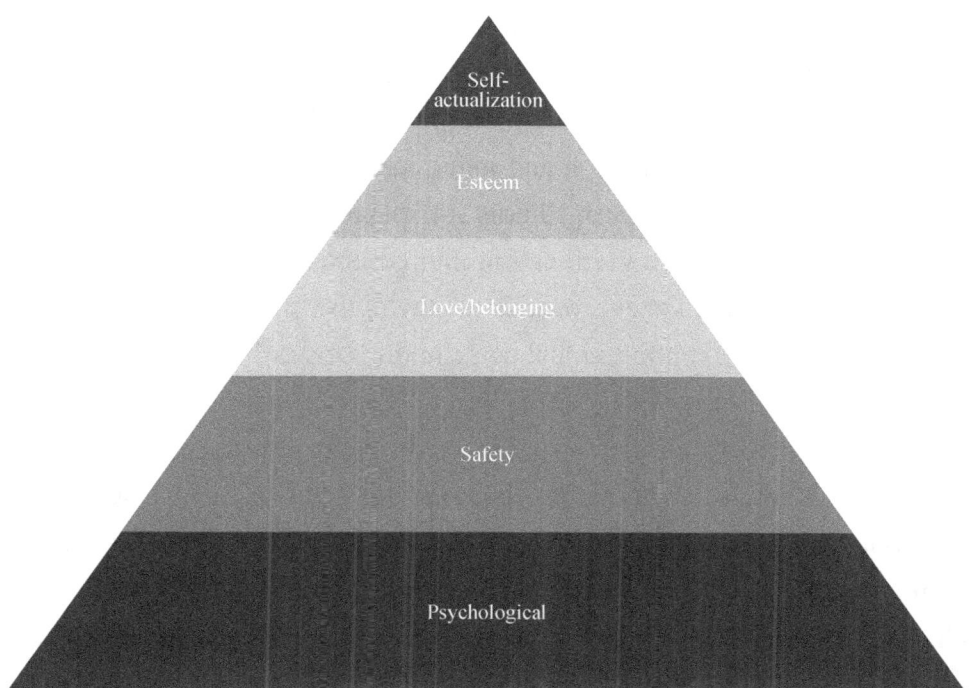

Regardless of our individual circumstances and experiences, we are all born with inherent skills, talents, and limitations. Examples may include levels of intelligence or physical abilities. This presents us with the realization and truth that each person is unique and multidimensional. It makes us who we are and even defines how we live.

While humans have the same basic needs, the ways in which we satisfy them are directly impacted by our own abilities. This leads to the following questions for consideration:

- What can we do to shape our lives, our futures, and, ultimately, our overall well-being?
- How can we make our journey more joyful, positive, and fulfilling?

According to a study conducted at the University of Illinois at Urbana-Champaign, the mean level of happiness across 43 nations, measured on a scale of 0 to 10 (0 = most unhappy, 5 = neutral, and 10 = most happy), was 6.33 (Diener & Diener, 1996). A similar study conducted that same year at the University of Chicago found that three in 10 people said they were "very unhappy," one in 10 claimed they were "not too happy," and the remaining six indicated they were "pretty happy" (Myers & Diener, 1996). In 2009, a study on satisfaction and individualism building on the original research from the University of Illinois at Urbana-Champaign found a direct relationship between life gratification and eccentricity (Diener & Diener, 2009). The challenge for everyone is to stay at the "very happy" level and create a future based on individual contributions toward their goals.

Regrettably, many assumptions are made about how one can achieve success. Humans often focus on their natural, societal, and institutional environments, leading to the belief that others should be responsible for their success. Realistically, the only person who can truly make a significant change to shape their future is themselves. All other conditions can and should be supportive and supplementary.

At birth, we are each given individual skill sets, aptitudes, and abilities. Ultimately, we are then responsible for how we use these to our advantage to attain success. Humans are capable of learning, as well as adapting. Like watering a seed, it is up to each of us to tap into our own potential. We must use our resources, challenge ourselves, and nurture our ability to learn. We must not limit ourselves. Instead, we must welcome every opportunity to grow.

For instance, although I've always enjoyed swimming and boxing, I had never considered myself a long-distance runner. In 2010, however, I decided to push myself and take on the challenge. Despite my lack of experience, I was determined to try something new—something that intimidated me. I registered for a half marathon in Florida and, after four months of incremental runs and strategic training, I increased my running distance from one mile to 10 miles. I was growing stronger both physically and mentally.

On the day of the race, the air was thick with humidity. My run was a blur of pounding feet and tired legs. It was, surprisingly, exhilarating. When the finish line came into view, a surge of adrenaline pushed me through. I managed to complete the 13.1 miles in less than three hours—30 minutes faster than the average finish time! My sense of accomplishment was overwhelming. The half marathon was more than a race; it was a testament to my perseverance and my ability to achieve my goal.

Sadly, some people choose not to challenge themselves, which hinders their personal growth. By avoiding new situations and opportunities, they miss the chance to learn and develop new skills. If they continue to stay within their comfort zone or a risk-free environment, they cannot reach new heights in their lives or careers. Their potential remains untapped.

So many of us are not fully aware of our capabilities. We often dismiss or underestimate the notion of challenging ourselves due to an unfounded fear of failure. The irrational fear may be deeply ingrained, founded in past experiences, pressures, or self-doubt. However, we must discover those inner talents and tap into our valuable energy through new ambitions. We must accept that we learn from both successes and mistakes. It is a shame to see so many young people living a life in which they never truly discover their powers or tap into their full potential. The sky is the limit!

I hope to inspire others through my own lessons and stories. I encourage others to look inside themselves, trust their abilities, and learn to push forward to become the best they can be. Achieving this isn't easy. It requires dedicated work—but it is possible. By embracing the challenges, nurturing our potential, and committing to growth, we can unlock incredible possibilities within ourselves. You need to embark on your own journey, knowing the rewards of self-discovery and achievement are well worth the effort.

Obviously, building a successful and happy life is not an easy task. Life presents obstacles, but we must run through the doors that are opened. These opportunities might be offered to us, earned through hard work, or created ourselves. However, if opportunities were simply handed to us, everyone would be successful! But working for your own success will enrich your character, provide a sense of accomplishment, and give you the tools needed for continued growth. By staying focused and committed, you can make the most of the opportunities that lead to success.

Jeff Bezos, for example, was not simply handed the opportunity to become a billionaire. Instead, he identified a need for an online bookstore, built the business from his garage, and invested endless hours to make his dream a reality. Today, the American entrepreneur is an investor, founder, and CEO of Amazon, one of the world's largest online global retailers. He's worth more than US$150 billion. However, he was certainly not handed the idea of starting an online bookstore and digital empire. Instead, he identified a need for such a business venture and decided to make the most of the idea, working long hours to make his dream a reality.

Realistically, opportunities vary across societies, geographic locations, and ability levels. In a poor or underdeveloped nation, it is more challenging to identify or create opportunities. Historically, however, extraordinary individuals have achieved unbelievable triumphs through resilience and determination, even in the face of significant challenges. For example, Mexican billionaire Carlos Slim Helú, a business magnate, investor, and philanthropist, generated tremendous success for himself in a society that, unlike much of the Western world, was not known as a land of opportunity. He earned every penny of his fortune through hard work. Today, he owns approximately 200 companies and is worth an estimated US$35.4 billion.

There are many examples of individuals who have overcome odds and limitations to achieve success. Obstacles come in many forms, including socioeconomic status, disability, gender, religion, cultural norms, race and ethnicity, language, geographic location, family responsibilities, and age. However, history has shown that many people around the world have risen above obstacles through hard work and determination, building a successful life despite all odds and limitations. Abraham Lincoln, for example, faced poverty and setbacks only to lead his country through the Civil War and work to end slavery. As a young man, Stephen Hawking was diagnosed with ALS. However, he defied the odds and became a revered theoretical physicist. And Oprah Winfrey overcame abuse and deprivation to build a media empire and become a well-known philanthropist.

Opportunities are available in many different forms. For instance, there are valuable chances to obtain an education from a high school, college, or community course. Regrettably, many individuals do not take advantage of these offerings. According to the U.S. Bureau of Labor Statistics (2024), 61.4% of high school graduates make it to college, but only 54% complete their degree (Nietzel, 2024).

Financial constraints are a significant hurdle to attending an institution of higher education. Still, there are ways to overcome them, such as securing student loans or scholarships for academic merit, athletics, or philanthropic commitments. I, however, do not advocate for the route of student loans because they can lead to significant debt burdens for graduates, making it difficult to pay off the principal and interest over time. This financial strain can take years to overcome, delaying important financial milestones. Personally, I worked numerous odd jobs, from washing dishes to driving a limousine, to support my educational goals and multiple degrees without accruing college debt.

I firmly believe that investing in education pays lifelong dividends, offering benefits beyond the classroom. It opens doors to better employment, higher earning potential, and personal discovery. The knowledge earned through education leads to a more fulfilling life, making every sacrifice along the way more worthwhile.

Achieving success demands focus and unwavering determination, underscored by meticulous long-term planning. You should not assume that luck is all that is needed to realize achievement. While a fortunate few may inherit wealth and privilege, most create their own paths to success through their unique skill sets and abilities.

As mentioned, a good college education is non-negotiable in terms of setting the first building blocks of a successful life. Unfortunately, many view college as merely a pathway to a career. However, the first 10 years after college graduation are critical when becoming established and creating success. A degree is more than an education—it is the first step in a journey that prepares you to work in a particular segment of the economy. It helps to expand your mind, becoming an analytical thinker who can evaluate information, identify patterns, draw conclusions, and solve complex problems. A comprehensive education affords you the privilege of identifying as a professional learner.

For instance, being a professional bodybuilder shares some parallels with being an undergraduate student. Both require years of dedicated training, honing one's craft, and working toward a goal without giving in to distractions. In bodybuilding, growth is evident in the size of one's muscles and physical abilities. In academics, it's reflected in one's grades and progression to new levels of intellectual challenges. Just as a bodybuilder refines their techniques and adopts a healthier lifestyle, students sharpen their skills and expand their knowledge. After four years, a student has learned to juggle four or five courses simultaneously. At the beginning of a semester, students know little about the subject matter. Then, after several months, they've learned enough from the course to pass a final exam. After repeating the process many times over the course of several years, the student becomes a professional learner. Like a bodybuilder working toward their fitness goal, the student has exercised their mind to reach a new level of potential.

And the potential of human abilities knows no limits. However, many people never fully explore their mental or physical capabilities. They choose to settle in their comfort zones, remaining unaware of the extent of their potential. For example, as an average swimmer, I was aware of my boundaries in the pool and had a good sense of my endurance level. Then, in 1992, during a summer boating trip in the Florida Everglades, my canoe capsized, plunging me into the deep waters below. Panic briefly seized me as I surfaced. With no lifejacket to buoy me, and the current dragging the canoe away, instinct took over. The distance between me and the canoe seemed insurmountable—at least 30 feet—but with each stroke, the gap narrowed. Before I knew it, my hidden ability kicked in and I was swimming much faster than I ever thought I could. After what felt like an eternity, my outstretched hand grazed the canoe and I pulled myself back on board!

I often hear all levels of professionals discuss the trials of their daily work, expressing confusion about their job expectations, grumbling about their workload, struggling to balance their work and personal lives, and scrutinizing their compensation. For many, the workday can become consumed by stress, anxiety, and negativity. Many do not embrace new tasks or view the confidence given to them by their superiors as a positive new encounter. They may feel weighed down by fear, doubting their abilities and feeling overwhelmed by uncertainties. This mindset can lead to a sense of stagnation within their organization. Instead, they could consider reallocating their time and initiating more flexibility within their personal schedules to achieve unexpected feats.

Success isn't merely a byproduct of earning a college degree. It requires perseverance when entering the workforce. Yes, a college education provides you with the chance to obtain a good job within your field; however, the real test begins after you take the job. Just as earning an A in school demands hard work and commitment, excelling in the job market requires continuous effort and a willingness to go above and beyond expectations. Unfortunately, many college graduates go from investing unlimited time in achieving the highest grade in their college courses to limiting themselves to being a 40 hour-per-week employee due to the perception of "normal working hours" established by most societies.

The 40-hour workweek is regarded as the standard for full-time employment in the United Sates. Various federal laws in the United States utilize this number as a threshold for full-time employee incentive programs. However, there are 168 hours in a week. Thus, if the expected average number of hours worked per week is set at 40 in most businesses and there are 168 hours in a week, the average person is spending less than a quarter of their time each week at work. This leaves more than 75% of the week for other aspects of life.

People often draw similarities between time and money because both are valuable resources that are finite and can be spent, saved, or invested. Obviously, there are a set number of hours in a day, and you can access only a certain amount of money in your bank account based on your budget. Regrettably, neither your time nor your money can miraculously multiply on its own. Allison Rimm (2018, para. 4), in "*Taming the Epic To-Do List*," argued that "time is a finite resource, but people rarely budget their time with anywhere near the rigor they apply to their finances." Rimm recommended a three-fold strategy to manage one's priorities. The first list includes non-time-sensitive projects, the second list is for items that must be completed that day, and the third list includes the not-to-do items (reminders of those things that aren't worth one's time). She also introduced calendar blocks to schedule specific tasks to complete within a certain period. All three lists should be reviewed at the start of each day to prioritize, organize, and maintain focus.

The practice of time management should apply to both your work and your daily life. For instance, eight hours a day of sleep equals 56 hours of sleep per week. Eight hours a day on meals, self-care, and activities like driving, shopping, and exercise equals 56 hours per week. Added together, it comes to 112 hours per week out of the 168 total hours. Thus, there are 56 hours per week left for productive work and creativity. However, if the remaining time is mismanaged, valuable time is wasted on activities like social media. In fact, studies have shown that young people, on average, spend 4.8 hours a day on non-educational social media platforms (Statista Research Department, 2024).

In a world where competition for excellence is fierce, it is up to us to identify our own strengths and weaknesses. We are not created equal; however, we are unique. True progress begins with self-awareness. With it, we gain the clarity needed to set meaningful goals and develop effective strategies to achieve them. Self-awareness is the driving force behind lasting change. Undoubtedly, we all want to better understand ourselves so we can perfect our strengths and overcome our weaknesses to compete with others.

At the beginning of each semester, I told my students that I could not possibly know who would be earning an A vs. an F. Instead, each student held the key to their own academic success. It was not just about attending class. It was about actively engaging in the learning process, putting in the necessary work, and managing time effectively. If, for instance, a student spent the average number of hours studying for exams, then they would likely receive a C, an average grade. However, if a student proactively assesseds their learning ability and, in turn, invested extra time to obtain a higher grade (like an A), then the concept of "normal" study hours would go out of the door.

Throughout your life—in whatever you do—you must set goals and be driven to invest time and effort to meet them. Therefore, you should not limit yourself to a set number of hours for study or work. Commit to whatever is necessary to reach your goal!

As I mentioned earlier in this book, I quit school at age 13 to help support my family by working in a high-end antique shop in Tehran. Quickly, it became obvious to me that earning an education was my one path out of such a life. Education became my life's goal, and, despite limitations, I managed to obtain my high school equivalency education and travel to the United States to pursue additional degrees. Although my friends in America were giving in to the many temptations of being a young adult, I funded my college tuition by working up to 70 hours a week. I was determined to keep up with my studies, achieve my goals, and have fun if I could find the spare time!

I learned early that learning how to study was a crucial skill. Developing strong study habits helped me absorb information and get good grades in high school. Then, I was better prepared for my college career. By mastering the art of studying, time management, and critical thinking, you, too, can invest in academic and professional success.

Remember, success transcends merely clocking in and out of one's job. While the hours worked are important, they are one piece of the puzzle for achieving recognition and accomplishment. In today's environment, you are competing against others who are striving for the same rewards and acknowledgement. Plus, the larger the company, the more challenging it will be to be recognized. In other words, just as all businesses must compete with their rivals to succeed, individuals working within an organization should view themselves as entrepreneurs or competitors striving for excellence in their field.

Thus, you should adopt an entrepreneurial mindset, where you take ownership of your role, your projects, and your career path. It is about delivering results, building relationships, and approaching tasks with enthusiasm and a positive attitude. By doing so, you position yourself not only for success but also for growth. Regardless of the size of the company or its type of business, a determined, positive mindset will eventually be recognized and lead to higher positions, greater responsibilities, and additional pay. After all, a job pays for an individual's cost of living, allowing them to set a strong foundation for a rewarding, sustainable life.

You should not limit yourself when aiming to attain financial security and success. During the critical years after college, you should hyper-focus on defining and reaching for your goals and objectives. Just like building a dream house, vision and planning are key to financial gain. Embarking on a college career is much like purchasing a parcel of land in a desirable location. Just as the land represents the foundation of the future dwelling, education provides the groundwork for your life. College, like the land, is a canvas full of opportunities, waiting for you to shape it according to your goals. Investing in your career requires dedication, akin to the labor and money invested in constructing a house. Moreover, a well-built home becomes an asset just as an education and hard work will yield dividends in your life.

Achieving your goal of creating a successful life requires a strong focus, prioritization and effective scheduling, and the courage to discover your underlying abilities. In doing so, you'll be better equipped to secure a larger share of life's rewards. If you practice these principles during the first several years after college life, you will discover your strengths and take advantage of your potential. Like an athlete who builds their physical and mental ability as they train, you can build self-esteem and gain experience through studies and diligent work. Anything is possible!

And just like Maslow noted in the hierarchy of human needs, your physical needs require financial stability and status. Then, you will be able to seamlessly address your other needs like love, belonging, and self-actualization. Financial stability may not guarantee happiness, but it undoubtedly plays a role in addressing certain aspects of life, particularly physical needs. With financial security, you can more easily acquire things that have price tags—whether it's securing housing, ensuring access to healthcare, or receiving a high-quality education.

Having financial resources also allows you to solve problems more efficiently. For example, unexpected expenses like car repairs or medical emergencies can be addressed without the added stress of financial strain. Moreover, much of society is influenced by financial status. Social structures, opportunities, and even relationships can be impacted by your social position.

During my third year of teaching at Penn State University, I was interviewed by a local newspaper about my career. As the reporter closed the interview, he asked, "Professor Khosrow-Pour, what is your equation for success?"

I answered:

Success = Intelligence + Hard Work + Determination + Commitment + Positive Attitude

While some people may be more intelligent, it doesn't necessarily mean they will be more successful. In fact, intelligence alone is not enough. Intelligence is amplified by setting clear goals, perseverance, and effective planning. These efforts will, in turn, enhance problem-solving skills and foster your creativity and vision.

Hard work is fundamental to success because it builds resilience, develops discipline, and creates opportunities. Even the most intelligent individuals cannot meet their goals without putting in long hours. For instance, Bill Gates, the founder of Microsoft and one of the most influential, richest men on earth had to work to get to where he is today. He devoted countless hours to writing codes, foreseeing the digital revolution, and structuring lucrative business deals.

Like running a marathon, physical preparedness and a determined mindset are driving forces that propel individuals forward. A sharp focus will help you overcome obstacles, maintain motivation, and reach your goals. Determined individuals are insistent on achieving their established objectives.

A committed effort and investment in self-improvement strategies are essential to accomplishing your goals. A strong sense of commitment prevents you from giving up when progress seems slow and enables you to persevere through setbacks.

Finally, maintaining a positive attitude helps you navigate challenges more effectively to achieve your desired outcome. Optimistic individuals can face adversity, empower others, and maintain a higher level of productivity. Regrettably, many people view things in a negative light, indirectly creating obstacles to accessing their hidden abilities. Obviously, we all deal with some limitations and challenges. However, you cannot let these troubles cloud your view.

By developing a comprehensive understanding of the elements within the equation for success, you can formulate effective steps to make thoughtful, deliberate decisions. By utilizing and practicing these strategies, you can accomplish even the most challenging goals and realize your full potential in life. While the journey may be hard, it ultimately spotlights your abilities and sets you apart, paving the way for personal and professional success.

References

Diener, E., & Diener, C. (1996). Most people are happy. *Psychological Science*, 7(3), 181–185.

Diener, E., & Diener, M. (2009). Cross-cultural correlates of life satisfaction and self-esteem. In E. Diener (Ed.), *Culture and well-being: The collected works of Ed Diener* (pp. 71–91). Springer.

Mcleod, S. (2024, January 24). *Maslow's hierarchy of needs*. SimplyPsychology. https://www.simplypsychology.org/maslow.html

Myers, D. G., & Diener, E. (1996). The pursuit of happiness. *Scientific America*, 274(5), 70–73.

Nietzel, M. T. (2024, February 1). Percentage of adults with college degrees edges higher. Forbes. https://www.forbes.com/sites/michaeltnietzel/2024/02/01/percentage-of-us-adults-with-college-degrees-edges-higher-finds-lumina-report/

Rimm, A. (2018, March 26). Taming the epic to-do list. *Harvard Business Review*. https://hbr.org/2018/03/taming-the-epic-to-do-list

Statista Research Department. (2024, November 22). U.S. teens average time spent on social networks per day 2023. https://www.statista.com/statistics/1451257/us-teens-hours-spent-social-networks-per-day/

U.S. Bureau of Labor Statistics. (2024, April 23). College enrollment and work activity of recent high school and college graduates summary [economic news release]. https://www.bls.gov/news.release/hsgec.nr0.htm#

Chapter 11
Freedom is not for Free

The desire for freedom is a fundamental aspect of human nature, rooted in our desire for autonomy. It represents an ability to live without restrictions or limitations. Ultimately, freedom allows individuals the opportunity to make decisions that align with their values, beliefs, and aspirations. It is a driving force behind many social movements and personal endeavors, reflecting humans' need to forge our own paths and live fulfilling lives.

However, with freedom comes the responsibility to respect the rights of others. Exercising your freedom should not infringe upon the rights of others. A balance is essential for maintaining a just society.

Regrettably, freedom is not equally available to all human beings around the world. In many societies, basic rights and liberties are severely restricted. Some countries are ruled by systems, institutions, or governments that limit speech, education, information, and travel. Freedoms may be removed to maintain control, exploit labor, stifle opposition, and perpetuate poverty.

In the Western world, stable democratic societies allow their citizens a high degree of personal and political liberties, including freedom of expression, speech, media, travel, and religion. However, these opportunities are often taken for granted, particularly by younger generations and those who lack an understanding of the historical struggles for freedom. In addition, people who are not exposed to other cultures around the world may not appreciate their own freedoms. Experiencing different lifestyles and societal norms can highlight the value of your own rights.

A common misperception in free societies, particularly capitalistic ones like the United States, is that by simply living in such a society, one automatically benefits from the different types of freedoms or choices it offers. A person who lives in a free society and sleeps on the streets is a citizen of that society. Thus, they should be able to live comfortably, eat nourishing foods, and access warm clothes. However, because that individual does not have the financial means, the benefits of such freedoms or choices are stripped away. The practical reality of their situation limits their ability to exercise their freedoms, paralleling the experiences of those living without freedom in repressive environments. Both face barriers that stop them from fully participating in their respective societies. They are merely trying to survive.

Those living in free societies should take advantage of fully enjoying their freedoms, especially those with non-material aspects. Examples include participating in civic engagement like voting, expressing yourself through art and music, pursuing enriching hobbies, and volunteering for causes you care about. Participating in a free society without restrictions is a valuable gift that many people around the world aspire to but may not have.

In a free society, you can express yourself without restrictions. However, it's important to realize that finances directly impact how much an individual can take advantage of the other freedoms and benefits available in society.

Freedom ranges from the ability to travel, choose where you reside or what kind of car you drive, to where or what you can eat, and what you can wear, what school you attend, what kind of medical treatment you receive. Still, financial freedom—another form of freedom—directly impacts almost every other freedom

Each of the freedoms mentioned above requires a key to unlock their use. If you look carefully at it, that key is inscribed with a dollar sign. If you cannot financially claim that key to unlock those freedoms,—then those rights are not truly available to you.

The relationship between financial ability or freedom and the full utilization of freedom's benefits within a free society is extremely important to benefit from the privileges afforded to the citizens of a free society. An individual living in a free society can have freedom of expression and other basic offerings; however, to take advantage of all the freedoms presented, they need the means: financial freedom.

Financial freedom is the ability to purchase both essential and non-essential goods and services, while also being able to meet other financial obligations. Unlike other types of freedoms, financial freedom is neither readily nor easily available to everyone. In most cases, it must be developed by the individual over time. Sometimes, an individual's financial ability is strong due to family and inheritance. However, most people must build their own financial security through time, knowledge, and commitment. It is a carefully planned process and execution. Once the financial foundation is created, the individual can begin to enjoy the fruits of that financial freedom.

For instance, there is a difference between possessing freedom and having the resources to access it. Accessing information might require purchasing a book or a digital device. Without these purchases, an individual may be limited in the types of information and knowledge they can obtain. Similarly, while an individual may have the freedom to travel, their ability to do so depends on their financial means to afford fuel, a passport, lodging, or airfare.

Another example is dining at an award-winning restaurant. While any individual is free to physically go there, they need the financial means to engage in the establishment's full range of services and menu items. You cannot necessarily say that you have the freedom to indulge in whatever you want at whatever place you desire. Yes, you might have the freedom to choose that restaurant; however, making a reservation and selecting anything from its menu requires financial means. If you cannot afford it, you have limited your freedoms. Unfortunately, this same scenario applies to many types of freedoms found within a free society.

Financial security also dictates major life decisions, such as whether to buy or rent a living space and the flexibility regarding the location or size of the property. It can impact the choice of school an individual can attend, the level of education they can afford, and their ability to go to good private schools or go abroad to pursue an education.

Investing a significant amount of money in education can be seen as a strategic decision that pays off in the long run. This investment often leads to greater earning potential and career opportunities. If an individual's wish is to obtain certain skills for a specific profession, they will have to have the financial means to do so. For instance, if you want to become a certified financial planner, you will need money to pay for the courses and materials, as well as to take the exams. Once you pay for access to this education, you can reach a point in which you will become a certified financial planner, thereby accessing a financially rewarding job.

In most free societies, in fact, a higher level of education is not free to all citizens. It is obtained or purchased. If an individual aims to attend an accredited medical school to earn a medical degree, they will need financial resources to pay for tuition, books, housing, and other expenses. Thus, pursuing higher education, although a freedom, is not an option for everyone due to the significant costs. This constraint can limit access to opportunities, hindering upward mobility as compared to a standard entry-level position.

Consider the entirety of what financial freedom offers and its relationship with what other freedoms, choices, or services within a society offer. Without financial freedom, you are denied certain services and opportunities. In many cases, you will receive the basic services and offerings available to you. This can significantly limit your quality of life. This may mean settling for minimal standards in housing, healthcare, and nutrition. It may prevent you from pursuing personal interests and hobbies, leading to a lack of fulfillment.

One example is if an individual has financial constraints and needs medical treatment but cannot afford an urgent care visit, does not have access to a high-quality medical facility, or cannot get assistance with medication costs. Not being able to afford or access proper care or delaying treatment can lead to serious, long-term negative consequences. A manageable condition might worsen without intervention. Inadequately treated illnesses can lead to complications and affect other parts of the body. Chronic pain will impact both the individual and their family, adding a burden to the household. It is a stark reality that even in a powerful country like the United States, many people cannot afford basic medical services like dental care, diabetes treatment, or blood pressure management.

Overall, quality of life can be drastically impacted by an individual's financial ability. As I stated, other than through luck or circumstance, financial freedom is most often built from a strong foundation. Regardless of how you attain it, you must be prepared to maintain and nurture your finances. If you do not, you cannot take advantage of the other rights that exist. Yes, it is a privilege to enjoy freedom and live in a society where you are free to share your point of view. However, if you can't take advantage of the benefits of the different freedoms within a free society, you are limiting yourself from creating a more comfortable, secure environment for yourself and your family.

Many people assume that having a general education or a steady job equates to financial freedom. However, these factors do not guarantee financial freedom. They are just elements that contribute to and sustain it. While having an income is essential for survival and a comfortable life, it may not be sustainable in the long term, especially if the job is terminated. Financial freedom requires more than a steady paycheck. It involves savings, investments, and financial planning to ensure long-term stability and security.

Regrettably, many people do not have a solid understanding of how to build sustainable financial freedom. They often assume, as I noted, that those who have money either inherited their wealth or got rich through some other means. While a small portion of the population is born into wealth or gets "lucky," most societies are filled with individuals who are "self-made." They relied on their will to succeed, with wealth being the by-product of their hard work and commitment to the goals they established for themselves at some point in their earlier lives.

It is interesting to study the trajectory of financially successful individuals. Phil Knight, co-founder and chairman of Nike (previously serving as its CEO), sold sneakers from the trunk of his car. Currently, he is worth close to US$40 billion. Steve Jobs, co-founder, chairman, and CEO of Apple, invested in a calligraphy class in college, which he said inspired him to focus on visually appealing designs and fonts made famous by Apple products. Richard Branson, founder of the Virgin Group, founded a magazine called Student at the age of 16. He used its success to launch a mail-order record business, which grew into Virgin Records. Martha Stewart, founder of Martha Stewart Living Omnimedia, worked as a model to pay for her college tuition before starting her at-home catering business. Other examples include Arthur Blank and Bernie Marcus, co-founders of The Home Depot; Tony Hsieh, CEO of Zappos; Blake Mycoskie, founder and chief shoe giver of Toms Shoes; Alexis Maybank and Alexandra Wilkis Wilson, fashionistas and co-founders of the Gilt Groupe; Mark Zuckerberg, chairman, chief executive, and co-founder of the social networking website, Facebook; and many more. These people share an entrepreneurial spirit and willingness to take risks. Through innovation and perseverance, they identified and exploited market opportunities to become successful entrepreneurs.

However, you do not necessarily need an earth-shattering idea—like Facebook—to create solid financial security. Stability does not mean being super rich. Many people compare their capabilities and chances of hitting it big to those highly noticeable successful people in society. In many ways, the media has promoted certain stereotypes of people with strong financial means. There are millions of people who have built a very strong financial foundation and freedom for themselves and their families without gaining celebrity status.

For example, David Barrett is the founder and CEO of Expensify, a software company that provides financial management tools. He chooses to keep a low profile, focusing on his family rather than publicity. Mark Pryor is a healthcare entrepreneur who founded and leads The Seam, a digital platform for the exchange of healthcare information. Finally, Rick Caruso is the founder and CEO of Caruso, a real estate development company known for luxury retail and other properties. While known in the real estate field, he maintains a low profile outside of his business initiatives. These entrepreneurs have made vital contributions to our society through innovation and knowledge. Still, they prioritize their business interests over seeking celebrity status.

As the saying goes no pain, no gain. Without a defined path and unshakable commitment, it is close to impossible to achieve lofty, long-term goals. Unfortunately, many people feel comfortable following the crowd, believing that simply living an average life will lead to financial success. However, achieving financial stability and prosperity often requires going beyond the conventional path and fighting for your share. It involves informed decisions, calculated risks, and seeking out opportunities that others might overlook.

Another misperception about accumulating wealth is the reliance on a full-time or part-time job as the only source of income. While it is critical to earn a consistent income, it is just as important to scrutinize how your money is spent. In other words, every dollar that is not spent should be viewed as a dollar that stays with the person. For example, profitable and sustainable businesses rely on both sales and robust cost management systems. Together, they create a strong net profit for the business, leveraging their strategies to maximize revenues and operational efficiencies.

In the same way, having a financial management plan can help you set achievable goals, pay off debt, build an emergency fund, utilize tax benefits, and secure your financial security. The concept and its practice are, therefore, suitable for any person interested in building a dynamic financial future. Unfortunately, many people want to live a glamorous life from the beginning. They want to "have it all" without understanding the value of a financial structure. A clear and well-defined plan serves as a roadmap that guides you through the complexities of life's many stages, enabling you to align your aspirations with practical steps that meet your evolving needs. Moving forward without a defined path is like driving thousands of miles between cities without a map. Just as a map or GPS uses coordinates to provide clear directions or shortest routes, a financial plan guides your financial decisions. It can help you identify options and certain sacrifices to achieve your goals. Just as you invest years of your time to earn a college degree, you will also need time and hardships to achieve a balanced financial future.

Many people believe that long nights of studying and countless hours of work are finished upon earning their college degree. Once they accept their first job, they assume they can have fun without considering their financial future. They prioritize enjoyment and avoid thinking about long-term financial planning. However, it is important not to let peer pressure and the desire to have fun deter you from making sound financial decisions. Many people lack the understanding that one cannot succeed in life without continuing to work hard, persevere, and stay committed to their efforts to attain financial stability.

While it is natural to want to enjoy life and celebrate newfound independence as a young adult, prioritizing your long-term financial health is crucial. In fact, balancing responsibility with enjoyment means you won't live paycheck to paycheck, constantly worrying about making ends meet. Plus, having certain freedoms through financial ability will provide experiences you may not otherwise have.

According to a survey, only 20% of American workers in their 20s save money, despite the average household income being about US$54,000 (Jackman, 2024). This clearly demonstrates that an overwhelming majority of young people do not invest in their future. Sadly, many of them believe that the government will provide financial support for them as they get older. This assumption can lead to complacency, with people relying on social security, pensions, or other assistance to ensure their well-being.

Learning to become an educated consumer is an important building block toward developing strong financial security. An educated consumer makes wise decisions when spending money, maximizing their return on investment. In addition, an educated consumer will not waste five dollars on a trendy cup of coffee. Instead, they'll brew a cup at home, saving several dollars per day and investing the difference in their savings. For example, if you save three dollars a day on coffee, you could easily save US$90 a month and US$1,000 dollars a year. That is a significant amount of money! Then, imagine investing those savings for 20 years! These cost savings would be from just one daily expense—imagine the savings you could achieve if you studied every expense through the lens of an educated consumer.

As discussed, individuals earn money in two ways: income and savings. Your goal should be to work hard to achieve your best income level. Simultaneously, you should strategically manage the money earned through your job (or jobs) in the most effective way.

When individuals choose to rent their living space, they spend between 30% and 40% of their income on housing. Unfortunately, many people believe that earning a good income means they should live in the best possible place, without understanding the ramifications of such a decision. For example, if an individual can save a minimum of US$500 a month by living in a safe, moderate neighborhood—even if it doesn't have all the amenities or luxuries one might prefer—then they could save as much as US$6,000 a year. Again, over 15 years, this could amount to a significant sum of money! Then, in a few years, the savings could be invested in a down payment on a property, turning the cost into a long-term source of income.

Later in this book, I will share a vibrant plan for how to achieve this goal, using my best practices for financial success. In fact, one's first investment in real estate could change the course of one's journey toward financial security.

As mentioned, many young people believe that accumulating wealth is impossible unless you are born into money or have a lucrative job or business. Yes, there is a certain truth to this assumption. But with careful planning and sacrifices, you can accumulate wealth.

In the first step to building your wealth after securing an education and employment, you must develop a disciplined plan to make the most of your income. You should not spend every penny of your earnings or assume that you will always have an income. This kind of mindset will get you nowhere fast, ensuring that you'll be living your life from paycheck to paycheck. Instead, you must commit to setting money aside from every paycheck to build a more financially secure future for yourself.

When I started my first full-time job at Broward Community College in Florida, I pledged to myself that I would put US$500 a month into my savings account. My annual salary was US$18,000 or US$1,500 a month. I also held part-time jobs in the evenings and on weekends, like cleaning tables in a restaurant, serving as a security guard, and driving cars. These brought me an additional US$1,000 per month. Altogether, my monthly income was US$2,500. I managed to live on US$2,000 a month and saved the remaining US$500. Like many people my age, I rented an apartment for US$800 a month. Other expenses included US$300 for utilities, US$200 for fuel, US$100 for insurance, and US$400 for meals.

Living within my means was an essential practice for maintaining my current and future financial stability. One way I managed this was by carefully watching my expenses. I would get my morning caffeine fix from McDonald's instead of the more expensive coffee shops. I also cooked most of my meals at home and drove a used car. I practiced the old saying: Every penny counts.

While living in Florida, I purchased a one-bedroom condo, putting down 20% of the purchase price and taking out a 30-year mortgage with a 7% interest rate. When I moved to Pennsylvania, I rented out the property for more than my monthly mortgage payment, providing me with an additional source of income.

My salary as an assistant professor in Pennsylvania was US$28,500. I followed the same lifestyle as in South Florida, and I continued to set aside at least US$500 a month in my savings account. By the end of my first year at Penn State, I had saved more than $20,000.

Then, I began thinking about purchasing a house close to the campus. In September 1983, I purchased a three-bedroom property in Chambers Hill, a suburb of Harrisburg within a 10-minute drive from the school. I supplied a 20% down payment and secured a 15-year mortgage for the remainder of the purchase price.

Later that month, Rachel and I moved into the new house. We stopped paying rent and, instead, made payments toward the 15-year mortgage. After working for two years, I was excited to own my own home (not a condo). I was living the "American Dream," joining the ranks of 65% of Americans who owned their own home in 1983 (Grall, 1995). Although 80% of my house was still owned by the bank—20% of its ownership belonged to me! Next, I was determined to build equity in the home, shorten the loan period, and pay less interest to the bank in the long run.

Most Americans choose a 30-year mortgage on the purchase of their home, paying the monthly fee according to the schedule calculated by their bank. I had taken out a 15-year mortgage on my second property, which increased my monthly mortgage payment as compared to a 30-year mortgage. However, the 15-year mortgage allowed me to save on interest and build equity quickly. If I had taken the 30-year mortgage, I would have had a longer loan term, made payments over a longer period, and accrued more interest over time. If I had continued paying only my regular monthly mortgage, I would have paid double the purchase price at the end of the 15 years. Thus, 50% more would have been paid to the bank for mortgage interest alone. However, if I had opted for a 30-year mortgage with a half-point lower interest rate, I would have paid three times higher than the purchasing price at the end of 30 years!

The 30-year mortgage option may be favored by the bank because borrowers end up paying more interest, which increases profitability for the bank. Regrettably, almost 95% of all mortgages are based on 30-year terms, in which the buyer takes 30 years to pay it off before they completely own the property.

However, many people do not realize or take advantage of the fact that the homeowner does not have to follow the normal pattern of paying off the mortgage in 15 or 30 years. Often, homeowners do not realize that their first property can serve as an asset for future investments, and, in turn, they can accumulate wealth through equity.

When I purchased my first home, I put down 20% of the purchase price and borrowed 80% of its value from the bank. If I could make an additional monthly mortgage payment, I would increase my share of the ownership and reduce the amount of interest I paid each month. This meant that more money from the regular mortgage payment would go toward the borrowed amount. Eventually, I started adding up to US$500 a month to the minimum monthly mortgage payment. The extra payments were applied to the principal amount of the loan, building my share of ownership and equity in the house.

Banks, in general, do not like to see their mortgage holders pay additional money toward reducing the principal amount. It, as I mentioned, reduces their chance of collecting the expected interest on the mortgage. At the time of signing the initial mortgage documents, I ensured there was no clause within the mortgage documents that would penalize me for additional payments.

By the end of my second year of home ownership, my share of its equity had grown to more than 40%, including the initial 20% down payment at purchase and the additional monthly payments strategically made toward reducing the borrowed amount. With such a strong ownership of the property, I wanted to make an additional investment. However, I needed access to cash for a down payment.

After an extensive search of local banks, I applied for a home equity loan based on the amount of equity I had in my first house. The bank approved my home equity loan for 75% of my 40% ownership in the first property. This meant I now had two mortgages: the original mortgage and the home equity loan. My plan was to continue making regular mortgage payments on the first mortgage while redirecting the additional payments I had been making toward the monthly payments to the home equity loan.

Next, I bought a three-bedroom townhouse, using the home equity loan as a 20% down payment. I took out a 15-year mortgage on the remaining value of the purchase price. This became my investment property. I found a tenant to rent the townhouse and began collecting US$500 more than my monthly mortgage payment for this investment property. I used the additional US$500 toward the principal to increase my equity in the investment property.

After two years, I had enough equity in the second property and applied for a line of credit similar to a home equity loan. In this case, the bank uses your property as collateral to lend you money. This is a safe practice for banks in the case of default because they can sell the property at market value to recoup their money.

I chose not to invest in stocks to make money because, at that time, the market was highly volatile, making it feel like a gamble rather than a secure investment. I preferred the stability of real estate investments, where I could tangibly manage and increase my equity through consistent rental income and property appreciation.

At that time, I was paying rent for the Idea Group, Inc. (currently referred to as "IGI Global Scientific Publishing") office space in Harrisburg. Rather than continue paying a hefty fee to the property's landlord, I decided to buy an office building in Hershey. I used my line of credit from the second investment property as a down payment and took out a 10-year mortgage for the remaining value. Then, Idea Group, Inc. (currently referred to as "IGI Global Scientific Publishing") began paying me rent as the company's new landlord.

The commercial rent on the newest property was significantly higher than my other property, helping me pay off the 10-year mortgage quickly. About three years later, I sold my one-bedroom condo in Florida for almost three times the amount of my initial payment. I applied its sale amount to pay off my newest mortgage on the commercial investment property. Between paying extra toward the mortgage that I took on the commercial property and the added funds from the sale of the property in Florida to pay off this mortgage, I managed to pay off the mortgage in under four years! I owned the property!

Over the next 20 years, I was very active in the real estate market, investing in properties in Pennsylvania, New York, California, and the Cayman Islands. My strong credit rating and robust portfolio of properties helped me secure a multi-million-dollar line of credit, which I used to invest in luxury properties. For example, I purchased a three-bedroom condo in Los Angeles for $1.8 million. The unit was eventually rented to a grocery chain chief executive. I used the monthly rent to pay off the money I had withdrawn from my line of credit. Later, I sold the L.A. property to a Chinese investor for US$2.85 million in cash, making a profit of more than US$1 million on the investment. The funds from the sale of the property paid off my entire line of credit, with the remaining funds placed into my savings account. That same year, I purchased a US$2.5 million property in New York City.

IGI Global Scientific Publishing, outgrew my initial commercial space, pushing me to invest in another property. I used cash to purchase two acres in Hershey, and took out a multi-million-dollar, 10-year mortgage to build a two-story, 20,000 square-foot office. IGI Global Scientific Publishing occupied part of the building, while the unused space was rented to other businesses. To support the construction of the building, I took out a multi-million-dollar mortgage with a 10-year term. With the rental income from all three businesses, I managed to pay off the mortgage on this building in less than five years.

Within just a few years after the company moved into this building, it grew significantly. Thus, Idea Group, Inc.'s (currently referred to as "IGI Global Scientific Publishing") headquarters needed more space. I, in turn, did not renew the lease of the other businesses once their initial contract expired. Idea Group, Inc. (currently referred to as "IGI Global Scientific Publishing") now occupied the entire building, becoming the only rent-paying tenant, with all monies directed to the owner—me.

After several years of making casual investments, my family now owns residential and commercial real estate worth millions. A large portion of the properties are used as rentals, generating close to US$ 1 million in revenue each year.

Learning about real estate investment involves understanding that it is a long-term commitment. Initial investments are required, including costs like taxes, closing costs, and legal fees, which means it will take time to recover these expenses. In addition, property values can fluctuate; however, this should not deter you from investing. It is crucial to invest within your means. You do not need a vast amount of money to start. The effort and initial costs are part of the process, which can lead to substantial rewards. Stay patient and focused on your long-term goals.

I started my journey in real estate with an initial US$10,000 in savings, which I achieved through self-discipline as I committed to setting aside US$500 a month in my savings account. This initial investment is, in fact, often the biggest challenge for many young people starting out. They may be hesitant because they are prioritizing instant gratification, living on a limited income, lacking financial education, or feeling uncertain about their job stability. Regardless, you must make some sacrifices to realize the bigger outcome.

As discussed throughout this chapter, a capitalist society like the United States offers various freedoms and choices. Examples include the right to choose what to wear, where to live, what kind of car to drive, and where to travel. Still, the many different types of freedoms are controlled by one's financial ability. In other words, your financial freedom is like a key you can use to unlock more freedoms.

It is false to assume that you must be born into money to enjoy financial freedom. Through careful financial planning and a certain level of sacrifice, you can accumulate wealth.

Remember, I came to this country with just US$150. Through hard work and an optimistic attitude, I put myself through college without student loans, earning an Associate of Arts in Business Administration, a Bachelor of Business Administration, an MBA, a Master of Science in CIS, and a Doctor of Business Administration. As a professor at Penn State University and the senior leader of my own scientific publishing company, I never stopped working. In fact, I practiced what I always preached: "Success = Intelligence + Hard Work + Determination + Commitment + Positive Attitude." In doing so, I was able to reach my goals and become a highly educated millionaire!

My first dream was to own a used bicycle. It symbolized more than just a means of transportation—it represented independence and the pursuit of my future. With a bicycle, I could explore new places with enthusiasm. Today, I drive a Mercedes Benz and a Porsche. I live in an affluent neighborhood in New York City. And I own rental and vacation properties throughout the United States and overseas worth millions. My childhood dream of having a bicycle drove me toward the freedoms and mobility I have today, allowing me to enjoy these luxuries and find happiness in my ability to proudly and confidently live my life of financial security.

References

Grall, T. S. (1995, October). Our nation's housing in 1993. United States Census Bureau. https://www.census.gov/library/publications/1995/demo/h121_95-2.html

Jackman, C. (2024, March 13). *Around 20% of Americans have no retirement savings, survey finds*. WCAX3. https://www.wcax.com/2024/03/13/around-20-percent-americans-have-no-retirement-savings-survey-finds/

United States Census Bureau. (1991, April). *Statistical brief: Homeownership in the 1980s*. Report Number SB/91-9. https://www.census.gov/library/publications/1991/demo/sb91-09.html

Chapter 12
Charity Work and Responsibility

As you enter the United Nations Headquarters in New York City, you will see the 13th-century poem Bani Adam (The Children of Adam) by famous Persian poet Sa'adi inscribed on the UN building entrance:

The children of Adam are limbs of each other,
Having been created of one essence.
When the calamity of time affects one limb,
The other limbs cannot remain at rest.
If you have no sympathy for the troubles and pains of others,
You are unworthy to be called by the name of a Human.

I heard this poem often while growing up in Iran. Today, it reminds me of my father's commitment to help others. Although he lacked strong financial resources, Dad always strived to provide for those in need. Without question, he paid his *Zakat*, an act of piety in which Muslims give a portion of their money to charitable causes. This obligatory act applies to Muslims in most countries as a form of worship. I clearly recall seeing a representative from the local mosque visit my father's shop to collect his share. However, I also vividly remember watching Dad unloading rice, cooking oil, dried vegetables, and other items from the trunk of his car to give to our struggling neighbors. He would tell me, "Mehdi, these people are less fortunate than us."

It was a simple yet profound act of kindness. Witnessing his generosity and random acts of kindness was important for me, teaching me the true value of compassion and selflessness. In turn, if I ever had financial means, I would try to help other unfortunate people of this world!

When I came to the United States, I learned that many good-hearted Americans support charitable organizations as a way to give back to their communities and contribute to causes they feel passionate about. They donate to a range of objectives, including medical research, disaster relief, and social issues. People also contribute because the U.S. tax system provides incentives for charitable giving.

During my early years of living in this country, I enjoyed volunteering at soup kitchens throughout Miami and Fort Lauderdale. I would perform various tasks to support the operations, including stocking shelves, arranging tables and chairs, and distributing food. After I moved to Pennsylvania, I continued to support a soup kitchen in downtown Harrisburg, providing financial contributions and helping serve meals on holidays like Thanksgiving and Christmas.

Financially supporting local non-profits was also important to me because it benefited my community by addressing pressing needs. In Pennsylvania, I supported the Bethesda Mission, a Harrisburg-based organization that offered services, shelter, food, and clothing to men, women, and children experiencing homelessness and poverty. I also contributed to the Make-A-Wish Foundation, a non-profit that grants a "wish" to children with life-threatening illnesses.

In the 1990s, while teaching at Penn State, I saw an advertisement in the campus newspaper seeking volunteers at Hershey Medical Center, one of the largest hospitals in the Harrisburg region. After contacting the hospital staff, my ex-wife, Beth, and I began volunteering in the gift shop on Tuesday and Thursday evenings. We would help the paid hospital staff sell things like gifts, children's toys, flowers, and greeting cards to patients and guests. We would wrap them with all kinds of colorful ribbons. We even got to wear a hospital uniform! It was an incredibly rewarding experience to know that, even though their loved one might be sick, we were able to offer a smile and a bit of comfort. We volunteered in the shop for two years until the gift shop merged with the hospital's bookstore within the Penn State College of Medicine.

As I would travel between my job at the antique shop and my GED classes in Tehran, I would often see people—even entire families—begging on the streets. Seeing a handicapped child and his father asking for help was an especially painful and memorable experience, serving as a reminder that behind every face is a struggle for survival. And I knew that I had a role to play in helping others.

Recognizing my own opportunities, I felt a profound responsibility to give back to my community and support the less fortunate. One day, I told myself as I rode my bicycle down the city street, I would have the financial ability to build a hospital for handicapped children in northern Iran. I wanted to support sick children and help to cure their illnesses. I hoped to make a meaningful difference in the lives of others and inspire change.

During a trip to Iran in 2000, I visited a small orphanage for handicapped children in northern Tehran. About 100 children were cramped into a 1,000 square-foot room. There was one nurse to look after the children and one doctor who visited on Wednesdays. Some of the children's hands were tied to the sides of their tiny beds, keeping them restrained. I was heartbroken.

For many years after my visit, I supported the orphanage through financial gifts, even helping to purchase an ambulance for the facility. Experiencing this transformative moment became the catalyst for turning my dream into a reality. At this time of my life, I had reached a point where I had the financial means, the necessary knowledge, and the important connections needed to pursue my next endeavor.

After speaking to my friend and attorney, Gary James, I began the process of setting up an organization that would help handicapped children in poor countries across the world. I analyzed numerous reports, case studies, and data to gain insights into their daily struggles, the various challenges they faced, internal policies, and the efforts of other humanitarian organizations.

In the 1990s, UNICEF and other international organizations began classifying children with only one parent as "orphans." Single parents in rural areas of developing countries often lack access to proper healthcare and, therefore, struggle to care for themselves and their children. Losing a parent can negatively impact a child's access to food, shelter, education, and healthcare, especially if the child is living with a disability. Losing the income of a parent, particularly that of the primary breadwinner, can be disastrous for a family.

According to some estimates, there are currently more than 240 million children with disabilities across the globe. Sadly, many of the illnesses that afflict children are preventable, including infectious diseases like AIDS. In addition, according to UNICEF and other organizations, it is estimated that there are tens of millions of orphans in third-world countries, with 25% being handicapped.

Handicapped children often face additional challenges when living in orphanages because the facility may not be equipped to meet the specific needs of children with disabilities. In many countries, like India and China, handicapped children and females are viewed as a financial liability due to cultural norms and economic conditions. The chance of such children being abandoned is extremely high. Many poor families in third-world countries cannot afford to care for a handicapped child, especially because the child will be unable to enter the labor market and help with family finances. As a result, the life expectancy of handicapped orphaned children in third-world countries is approximately 13 years of age.

Culture can also significantly impact how people view a handicapped child, shaping attitudes and behaviors toward those with disabilities. In some cultures, disabilities lead to social exclusion, discrimination, and limited access to healthcare or education. Once, I traveled to Port-au-Prince in Haiti, one of the poorest countries in the Western Hemisphere, with nearly 60% of its population living below the poverty line. The main purpose of my visit was to personally assess an orphanage for handicapped children. The facility, which housed about 150 children, was far below any standards for safety and cleanliness. In Haitian culture, view toward handicapped children vary based on education, social status, and religion. In fact, some Haitians see disabilities as having a spiritual cause and as a curse of God, leading to stigmatization and social exclusion (including getting rid of the disabled child)!

Then, in 2003, to do my part to address this global issue, I formed the World Forgotten Children Foundation (WFCF), a non-profit private organization that supports the health and welfare needs of children with disabilities. WFCF envisions a world where no child goes without the medical and therapeutic help and equipment they need—a world that utilizes sustainable practices in communities for the benefit of all.

In November 2006, I wrote an editorial feature in the WFCF newsletter called "Axis of Goodness," referring to the three pillars of kindness and compassion around the world: Supporters, Facilitators, and Providers. I defined these pillars by immersing myself in my non-profit work and observing what truly works to effectively help others. They include:

- **Supporters**: Supporters or "Financiers of Goodness" refer to those who provide assistance like monetary funding, tangible goods like clothing and food, expertise like medical assistance or engineering, and other forms of aid. There are countless numbers of people willing to serve as regular supporters or aides in the wake of disaster.
- **Facilitators**: Facilitators or "Agents of Goodness" are individuals or organizations that connect the efforts of supporters and providers. The role of the facilitator is to obtain the assistance provided by supporters, and, in turn, work with providers to offer services to those who need support. Many non-profit groups, as well as government organizations, act as facilitators.
- **Providers**: Providers or "Deliverers of Goodness" are those who advocate for and deliver the services supplied by supporters. These individuals are the "boots on the ground," volunteering regularly at facilities or delivering relief to disaster victims.

Every level within the Axis plays a meaningful role in contributing to important humanitarian work. Undoubtedly, all three pillars are needed in conjunction to deliver good work. It is then up to an individual to decide which level fits their skill level and availability. At times, you may serve at more than one level or find yourself acting as a "Mother Teresa" within all three roles. For instance, the UNESCO fulfills both the Supporter and Facilitator roles.

The more people who become involved in the Axis of Goodness system, the more good work can be delivered. In turn, we can work as partners to create a kinder, more compassionate place to live. So, the next time you donate to a non-profit, volunteer to assist a charity, or participate on a committee, remember that you are an active participant in the Axis of Goodness!

Once I formed WFCF, I was eager to dive into our work. With enthusiasm, we set out to make a tangible impact, fueled by my commitment and passion to pursue this cause.

In 2003, the organization partnered with the Dokimoi Ergatai program at Messiah University, a Christian university, to provide US$1,500 to Handicapées en Avant, a French charity group in West Africa, toward the purchase of 10 hand-powered tricycles designed to give physically disadvantaged children more mobility. In addition, WFCF awarded US$250 to the program for the purchase and delivery of visual assistance items for computers to support children with visual impairments. The following year, WFCF assisted the program with building solar-powered wheelchairs for those children who could not operate manual wheelchairs. The motorized wheelchairs were transferred to West Africa, where they were assembled on-site by student volunteers from Messiah University.

By 2005, WFCF, which was fully funded by my family, was actively seeking projects to amplify its support of orphaned handicapped children in poor countries. We often relied on larger, more established organizations like the United Methodist Church to identify trustworthy projects to fund. In turn, WFCF could act as the Provider to deliver the support to those in need.

That same year, WFCF worked with the Ukraine Peace Foundation, assisting two orphanages for handicapped children in Ukraine through US$1,000 contributions toward the purchase of nutritional and medical products. The money, which was allocated to the Zgurovka Orphanage and Bovarka Orphanage, was dispensed through the Ukraine Peace Foundation, who then monitored the appropriate use of the funds within their country. The following year, WFCF provided US$2,000 in cooperation with the Cancer Recovery Foundation International to fund chemotherapy, radiation treatments, and surgical procedures for disabled and orphaned children through the Ukraine Peace Foundation.

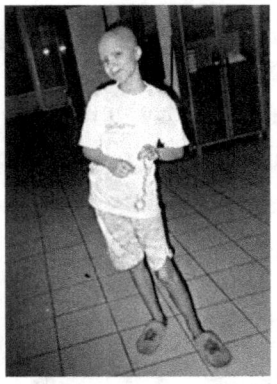

WFCF funded $2,000, in cooperation with the Cancer Recovery Foundation International's matching fund of an additional $2,000, to the Ukraine Peace Foundation to provide chemotherapy, radiation treatments, and surgical procedures for disabled and orphaned children.

In 2007, WFCF collaborated with Mercy & Sharing, a Colorado based non-profit group that operates orphanages for handicapped children in Haiti. As noted, with a population of nearly 12 million people, the Caribbean country faces ongoing challenges related to political instability, economic struggles, and natural disasters. WFCF provided US$2,860 toward the purchase of eight wheelchairs, which were bought in Miami and shipped to Haiti. When Mercy & Sharing asked our organization for additional funding for wheelchairs, the WFCF board of directors asked me to travel to Haiti to visit their largest orphanage for handicapped children. I was met by a representative of Mercy & Sharing, who provided me with a guided tour.

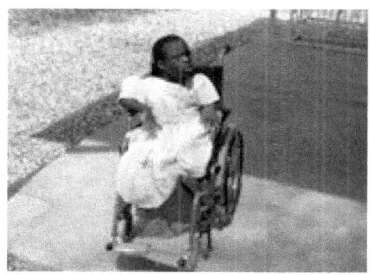

WFCF assisted MSF by providing $2,860 for the purchase of eight wheelchairs for orphaned children in Haiti.

The orphanage was appalling and inhumane. Sadly, the children were kept in a small room with urine-covered cement floors. They slept in bunkbeds piled three bed highs. After an extensive (and heartbreaking) tour, I asked the head of the facility to show me the original wheelchairs we'd provided to them. I wanted to see how they were used. Regrettably, they could not show me even one wheelchair. I was told by a friend who grew up in Haiti that the chairs were probably sold on the black market, with the money pocketed by facility officials.

The following year, the Russian-based Diema's Dream Foundation requested financial, medical, and educational support for physically and mentally disabled children. After extensive research about the organization and its credibility, WFCF learned that the foundation was founded in 1998 by the wife of a former U.S. ambassador to Russia and named after a handicapped Russian girl. Initially, the WFCF board approved Believe Project funding in the amount of US$6,000 to purchase 10 wheelchairs. A few years later, we contributed more than US$12,800 to Diema's Dream Foundation's Believe Project for verticalization orthopedic and physical therapies, as well as life skills services for orphans living with severe mental and physical disabilities. The Believe Project gives orphans who have multiple and profound disabilities the courage to believe they can see their world while standing on their two feet. We funded these services and equipment at the Elat'ma Orphanage in the Ryazan region in western Russia. The orphanage housed 96 children between the ages of two and 10.

 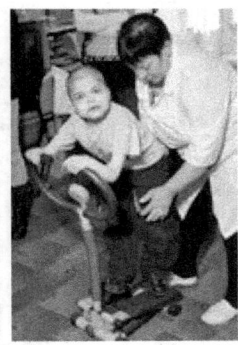 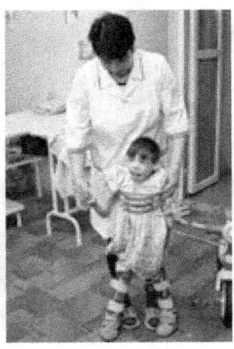 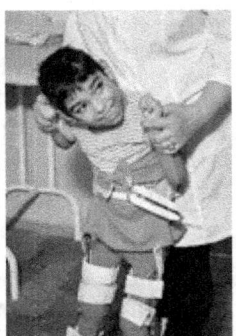

WFCF was also proud to collaborate with the African Community Project, operating out of the U.S. state of Washington. Initially, our organization provided the African Community Project with US$1,235 toward the purchase of beds, mattresses, blankets, pillows, and bed linens. Subsequently, WFCF contributed US$5,300 toward the Handicapées en Avant School in Burkina Faso, West Africa, for the acquisition of drawing boards to create relief drawings, Braille writing tablets, and other educational materials to support blind orphaned children. In addition to these projects, WFCF funded equipment and medical supplies in the amount of US$6,564 for the Center of Mobility and Stimulation of Children with Disabilities in Abidjan on the Ivory Coast. The project was managed and coordinated by the International Catholic Child Bureau in Brussels, Belgium, which aims to help children in Africa develop by promoting their dignity and enforcing their rights.

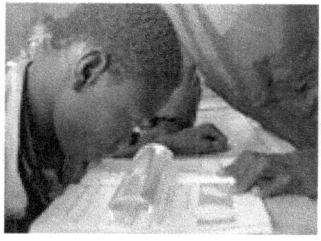

In 2009, a member of the WFCF board read a story in the *Los Angeles Times* about the Baby Box project in South Korea. This initiative was established in 2010 by Reverand Lee Jong-rak to save abandoned babies. The creator designed a box for mothers to place their unwanted babies in locations like public restrooms, serving as a safer alternative to leaving the child in dangerous conditions or cold weather. The Baby Box Church—the Jusarang Community Church—in Seoul now serves as a care facility for unwed mothers and babies, and Baby Box continues to be heavily utilized.

On average, more than 200 babies are left at the Baby Box Church facility each year. The shelter looks after the new arrivals for a few days before moving the children to orphanages as they await new families. WFCF initially provided US$1,600 to repair the cement stairs leading up to the shelter's box (a temperature-controlled chamber built into the wall). The following year, through a very generous donation from the Hyojin Kim Nirav Patel Foundation to WFCF for use at the Baby Box Church, US$4,378 was allocated to fund critical building repairs, including waterproofing interior and exterior walls and installing safety handles on a stairway leading to the baby room. Later, funding of US$4,087 supported the installation of cameras, the replacement of doors, and updates to the walls and windows.

To control the population, some countries limit the number of children permitted within each family. In 1949, China began promoting the use of birth control and family planning with the establishment of the People's Republic. Their efforts remained sporadic and voluntary until after the death of Chairman Mao Zedong in 1976. By the late 1970s, the country's population was rapidly approaching the one-billion mark, and its new leadership, headed by Deng Xiaoping, was seriously considering ways to curb its growth rate. in 1978, the leadership announced a voluntary program that encouraged families to have no more than two children, with one child preferred. By 1980, the central government sought to standardize the one-child policy nationwide. The one-child policy eventually ended in 2015, and, in 2016, the number was increased to three children per family.

The one-child policy, however, produced consequences beyond the goal of reducing population growth. Most notably, the country's overall sex ratio was skewed toward males, with upwards of 4% more males than females. Traditionally, male children, especially firstborn, are preferred, as sons inherit the family name and property, as well as care for their elderly parents. When most families were restricted to one child, having a girl became highly undesirable, resulting in a rise in abortions of female fetuses (made possible after ultrasound sex determination became available), increases in the number of females placed in orphanages or abandoned, and even infanticide of baby girls. Many Chinese families also started viewing handicapped children, both males and females, as undesirable. Thus, handicapped newborns were often abandoned at orphanages that were ill-equipped to meet these children's special needs.

As a result, many girls and handicapped children were adopted by families in the United States and other countries. Charity groups across the globe were also becoming involved in supporting Chinese orphanages. One of these organizations, the International China Concern (ICC) in Vancouver, Canada, began working with WFCF in 2016 when the foundation funded an ICC project for US$10,227. Together, the organizations provided custom sleep aid systems for 20 handicapped children to improve their physical and emotional health and decrease deaths by providing equipment that supports correct sleep positioning. The project also helped handicapped children participate in community activities, enhancing their social and emotional health, self-esteem, independence, and communication. The following year, WFCF supported ICC with an additional US$11,155 for the purchase of shower chairs, advanced shower stands, a walking frame, and wheelchair upgrades. Subsequently, in 2020, WFCF contributed more funding to ICC for the final phase of their project, securing additional mobility equipment for children with disabilities in China.

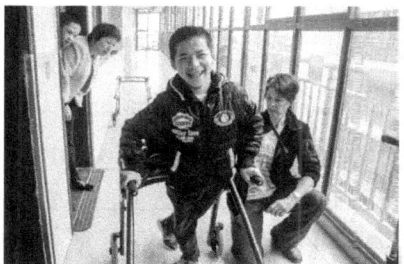

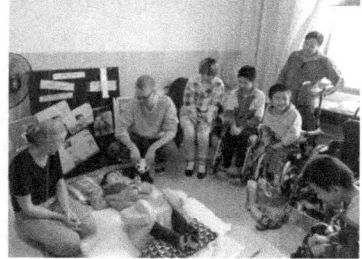

In 2020 and 2021, COVID-19 had a profound impact across the world, particularly in poor countries. Although the Western world could eventually access the COVID-19 vaccination, it was not available to the poorest countries. To support the millions of people impacted by the virus, WFCF contributed US$4,000 to the Kocebuka Community Foundation in Zambia, providing isolated families with ongoing awareness education and prevention programs.

Eventually, the Kocebuka Community Foundation, in collaboration with local government agencies, ministries, education boards, and WFCF, initiated a project to provide COVID-19 vaccination throughout Zambia.

 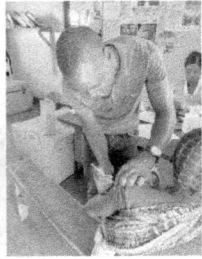 

Many experts strongly believe that play improves the cognitive, physical, social, and emotional well-being of children and young people. Through play, they can learn about the world and themselves. They also refine vital skills for studying, work, and relationships.

The Power of Play, a Canadian-based organization, provides sustainable playgrounds to children in poor countries. Their mission is to support every child's right to learn and develop through the power of play. The organization was founded by Reza Marvasti, an Iranian-born Canadian. The Power of Play employs locals for roles like project coordinator, carpenters, laborers, and volunteers. In 2021, WFCF provided US$6,000 to support the Power of Play's playground project at Nile Orphan Care in Juba, Sudan. Then, in 2023, WFCF contributed an additional US$6,300 to build a sensory playground for children in the Maasai community of Tanzania.

Approximately two billion people on the planet lack access to clean water. More than 800 children under the age of five lose their lives each day to diarrhea caused by contaminated water, poor sanitation, and unsafe hygiene practices. Furthermore, a staggering 1.5 billion people live without adequate sanitation (Kashiwase & Fujs, 2023; World Health Organization, 2024; World Vision, n.d.).

Organizations like UNICEF argue that the cost of running an orphanage is much higher than the cost of providing services to keep families together. In addition, it is more beneficial in the long-term for children to be raised within a family or community unit rather than an institution. Therefore, it is imperative that we provide programs that pull families and communities out of poverty to relieve the global orphan crisis, consider the overall well-being of children, and promote family stability.

Recognizing the urgency of this crisis, the United Nations has set its 2030 Agenda for Sustainable Development. Goals focus on areas like clean water, health and well-being, gender equality, sustainable communities, and partnerships. Only through collective efforts can we hope to alleviate the suffering caused by this global water and sanitation crisis.

In the fall of 2021, WFCF partnered with the African Community Project to fund a unique water management program that enables underprivileged communities in rural Africa to use water for sustainable practices like growing vegetables and other commercial crops to eat and sell, with money earned used to help maintain the upkeep of the initiative. The project also added chickens and farm animals to enhance its products. In total, WFCF contributed US$12,000 to drill deep into the ground to locate and access water and install a solar-powered water system for the Republic of Hope's Bulangzi Garden and Orchard Complex in the Zimba District in the Southern Province of Zambia.

WFCF has now expanded its mission to include community development as a part of its mission. This was important to our non-profit leadership because we also wanted to contribute to building stronger, healthier, more vibrant communities. The current mission statement of the organization is as follows:

The WFCF is a private non-profit effort, founded for the sole purpose of supporting projects that promote the health and welfare needs of underprivileged communities and orphaned children with disabilities in developing countries.

Engaging in charitable work is easier than many think, and if everyone contributed, our collective efforts could assist people from all backgrounds and places around the world. In turn, the world would be a better place to live. Just as WFCF believes in providing helping hands to less fortunate people of the world, charitable work is an essential way we can serve others and foster compassion. Let's not forget, we are all part of one human race and it is each of our responsibilities to assist others.

It is unacceptable that in a world where so many of us have ample food and resources, there are still people starving, suffering, and in desperate need. There are many ways we can help to alleviate the world's hunger and inhumane conditions. The disparity highlights a critical issue that demands our attention and action to ensure everyone has access to the necessities of life.

As mentioned in this chapter, Supporters provide financial assistance for different causes, Facilitators include individuals or organizations who work to deliver nutrition or services, and, finally, Providers are the individuals on the ground making everything happen. One can participate in one or multiple capacities.

Chapter 13
Summary and Lessons Learned

On the morning of June 18, 1951, a baby boy was born to a young, poor couple in Langarood, a village in the Gilan Province in northern Iran. The boy, Mehdi, shared a name with the 12th disciple of the Prophet Muhammad in the Shiite sect of Islam.

I am that little boy.

Like many other kids, I was the child of a young couple. My parents had four other children. They lost two of them: a boy at birth and a girl at six months old due to accidental suffocation. Eventually, they had two more boys.

I was right in the middle—the "forgotten child." As a middle child, I faced a unique set of experiences. Sometimes, I felt like I did not receive as much attention as my siblings. I also developed a strong sense of independence and resourcefulness. Above all, I developed skills in adaptability, as I was able to navigate many different situations.

My father worked hard to provide for his family and seek out financial opportunities. When I was six months old, our father moved us to a poor neighborhood in Iran's capital city, Tehran. Once there, our seven-person household shared a duplex with another family. Our portion of the duplex had two bedrooms, a kitchenette, and a small living room. The communal toilet (without showers) was in a shed in the yard, and we showered in a public bathhouse every two weeks.

My family's last name was assigned to us when the Iranian government implemented a modernization policy requiring everyone to adopt a surname during the early 20th century. Back in 1919, the government decided to issue birth certificates to all Iranian citizens, particularly those who lived outside of the bigger cities. My father did not have a formal birth certificate or a last name. He was known as "Son of Ali," with Ali being the name of his father. When he went to apply for a birth certificate, the government official originally gave us the name Khone Kabotor (blood of pigeon), but we later changed it to Khosrow-Pour (son of king) because kids at school would make fun of the last name.

My first life trauma occurred when my mother died in her early 30s. I was just 11 years old. She had been diagnosed with jaundice when, in fact, she was battling a life-threatening genetic blood disorder called GP6D. The doctor had prescribed her medications to treat the jaundice. Regrettably, those same medications were among those that would complicate the effects of the GP6D. I, too, have the same disorder and must, therefore, be careful when taking certain medications.

Dad was only 34 when my mother passed away, and he never stopped loving her. Eventually, he remarried an older woman. Although he was still young, he decided to marry someone who was not too young because my sister, Zari, was already 16 years old.

Prior to losing my mother, Dad owned a small business with his partner, Mr. Zaferaian, in Tehran's bazaar. Mr. Zaferaian could read and write, so he took care of the accounting. However, my dad found out his partner was cooking the accounting books Eventually, Mr. Zaferaian ran off, leaving my dad in debt to the farmers who had provided the store with rice and dried goods. Soon, Dad managed to find a job working as a salesman for another business.

One of my most memorable birthdays was in 2002 when my dad was visiting my family in the United States. During my birthday celebration, he told me that my birth certificate, which listed my birthdate as June 18, 1951, was wrong. In fact, I was born on June 18, 1952. In the old days, children could not start the first grade until they were seven years old. However, many Iranian families wanted to have their children to start school at age six. Therefore, Dad worked with government officials (that is, paid them off) to change my birth certificate, allowing me to enter school a year earlier than I was allowed.

The second trauma in my life occurred after losing my mother. With my dad working long days away from home, he instructed my older brother, Ali, to be the disciplinarian. On the surface, this made a lot of sense. Ali was, in fact, his oldest child (seven years older than me). Naturally, the oldest would assume the leadership role in the house if Dad was gone. Unfortunately, my brother took his role to an extreme, hitting us with his belt for minor mistakes and making us cower in fear for minor errors on our homework. Instead of being a pillar of support after our mother's death, my brother betrayed my father's trust. And we children paid the price. Shortly after, I began suffering from severe migraines.

This abuse happened on a regular basis. It is also why I experienced dissociative amnesia, causing this period of my life to be a blur. Still, the amnesia acted like a protective covering, shielding me from harm.

After Dad remarried, we moved into my stepmother's house in central Tehran. The house was old, an inheritance to my stepmom and her two sisters from their father. We lived on the side of the house with two bedrooms and a den. Several other people also lived in the house. My stepmom's younger sister lived on another side of the house. Her older sister lived in a bedroom in the basement. And the other tenants, Mr. Amir Karimi, his wife, and their young child, lived in the one-bedroom section of the house.

The kitchen was in the basement and was shared by all of the home's occupants. The home's one bathroom was in an outside shed. There was no shower or heat inside the shed. We used public bathhouses for our showers, a common practice in those days. Having showers and bathrooms inside one's house was a luxury, available only to elite and wealthy families in the influential neighborhoods of Tehran.

Shortly after we moved into my stepmom's house, an event changed the direction of my life.

One day, the other tenant, Mr. Karimi, was arrested for stealing from his employer, an antiques salesman named Mr. Javadi. Mr. Javadi sold bronze statues, great paintings, and Persian rugs. Many of his items were priced at $10,000 or more. Needing to replace Mr. Karimi, Mr. Javadi hired me for the summer. At age 13, I was hired to vacuum carpets, sweep, wash the tiled floors, and wait on customers.

Unexpectedly, at the end of that summer, Dad told me he needed my financial help in support our family. Thus, he could not afford to let me go back to school. Although I was devastated by the idea of quitting school, I did not want to disappoint my father or go against his decision. Instead of returning to class, I continued working full-time at the antique store.

The Iranian educational system would not allow students to quit their full-time schooling only to immediately begin taking GED courses. Per the old system, you had to wait a minimum of one year before signing up for the GED exam. This was to deter students from dropping out in the first place.

As I worked for Mr. Javadi, I began doing a lot of soul searching. Did I want to pursue the life of a shopkeeper? By the end of my first full-time month of employment at the antique store, I'd made up my mind: I would do whatever it took to pursue my education. It was the only way to change the trajectory of my life.

At the end of the one-year probationary period, I registered for evening GED courses to prepare for the ninth-grade GED exam. My workdays began at seven in the morning. After dinner, I'd head to my evening class. Then, I would study with my friend, Hossein, into the early hours of the morning. Regardless of what time I returned home, my dear grandmother was waiting to welcome me with dinner. Finally, my grandmother and I would fall asleep next to my two younger brothers, Mohammad and Ahmad, in our small den. We all shared a mattress on the floor. After the loss of my mother, my grandmother was always a loving support system for me.

I was careful to save the money that remained after contributing to the family funds. Mr. Javadi paid me six tomans a day, equivalent to almost US$1. My total pay was 180 tomans, with which I gave 100 to my dad to help with the family finances. I paid 60 tomans to the GED school, which left me with 20 tomans for food and other expenditures. Sometimes, I made an additional 50 tomans a month from customer tips for carrying rugs and other antiques to their cars.

Even with my limited income, I managed to buy my first used bike at age 15. I would ride it to work in the morning, to school in the evening, to my friend's house to study at night, and then back home. The bike gave me freedom and mobility. It was like I was riding on the clouds.

This was a tough period in my life. I didn't even have enough money left to purchase necessities like clothes for the winter months. One day, Mr. Davood, a regular customer at the antique store and a friend of Mr. Javadi, asked me why I was not wearing a warm coat in the frigid weather. I tried to assure him that I was warm, but he saw me shivering. With much generosity, he handed me 100 tomans and instructed me to buy myself a warm coat—which I did! His actions taught me the concept of "random acts of kindness" and greatly influenced my personality.

After four years of working at the antique shop and going to school, I earned my high school diploma and prepared to take the national entrance exam for higher education. Regrettably, I was not admitted to my desired programs within the top universities for my desired areas of focus: medicine or engineering. I was only accepted at the Tehran University School of Cinema and Dramatic Arts. Plus, I would have to wait six months to start the program. Instead, I joined the Iranian army, knowing that, upon completion, I would pursue my education in the United States.

Like Sameed Behrangi's book, *A Little Black Fish*, I was eager to leave the familiarity of my home and explore the world. When I joined the army, I was 19. Like they say, I joined the army "as a boy and came out a man." Realistically, I was mature for my age because I'd started working at 13 years old. During that time, I had already learned about various aspects of life, particularly that you set your own destiny!

By the fall of 1973, I finished my two-year mandatory military service in the Iranian army. With my military discharge documents in hand, I applied for my passport. On December 6, 1973, I flew to the United States with my former classmate, Hossein, and arrived in Washington, D.C. We stayed in the city for two weeks before moving to Miami to attend English language services classes and, eventually, Miami-Dade Community College.

As a foreign student, I was required to pay my tuition before the start of each semester. In addition, I was not eligible for loans or any kind of financial assistance. As a result, I was living on a very tight budget and relying on cheap meals like McDonald's French fries!

Immediately after arriving in Miami, Hossein and I began searching for jobs. I ended up working as a busboy at a Chinese restaurant.

In 1974, I enrolled in Miami Dade Community College for electrical engineering before changing my major after one semester to business administration. Unsurprisingly, I was the only Iranian student attending Miami Dade who was not majoring in the field of engineering! It took me just 15 months to finish the program, and receive my associate's degree in arts.

My first taste of racism in America happened in the summer of 1974. While I was riding my bike home from work on Biscayne Boulevard in Miami, a car pulled up next to me. One of the car's passengers threw his alcoholic drink in my face, shouting "Go home, f*ing Mexican." Then they sped off. It was a sad awakening for me to realize that racism exists in America, and, regrettably, this incident was not the last.

Before completing my associate's degree at Miami-Dade, I began searching for a four-year program to obtain my bachelor's degree. There were several strong programs across the country that accepted my application, including San Diego State University, the University of Alabama in Huntsville, and the

University of Miami. Ultimately, I chose the University of Miami because the school allowed me to transfer almost 95% of my courses from Miami Dade toward a bachelor's degree in business administration. Plus, I did not have to move out of state.

I began the academic program at the University of Miami in the fall of 1975. The school, at the time, was considered the second most expensive school after Harvard. To afford tuition, particularly for foreign students like me, I needed to work two jobs—a valet at the famous Fontainebleau Hotel five nights a week and a waiter on the weekends. I was also taking the maximum number of credits—18 credits or six three-credit courses.

Even while working almost 90 hours between my courses and jobs, I finished my bachelor's program in only two years, graduating in August 1977. I was proud to receive my Bachelor of Business Administration, majoring in business management and minoring in accounting.

Upon completing my bachelor's degree in Miami, I began searching for a graduate program. I was accepted into the MBA program at the Florida Institute of Technology in September 1977. However, before moving to the school in Melbourne, I embarked on a cross-country trip with two friends.

Each stop along the way offered new adventures and learning opportunities, from the bustling cities to the serene countryside. Moreover, the experience was deeply inspirational. We transported private cars for customers, first from Miami to St. Louis, Missouri, and then a different car to San Francisco. We also spent a few days in Las Vegas before driving another customer's car back to Hartford, Connecticut. The final leg of the trip required us to drive a car from Hartford to West Palm Beach, Florida. The agencies that transported the cars allowed us to drive free of charge. The customer was charged for the safe delivery of their vehicle to their desired location. The only costs we covered were fuel and transfer fees. In most cases, the owners of these cars also tipped us!

I finished my program in 11 months and, by August 1978, received my MBA with a major in finance. I even maintained a strong GPA—almost 4.0! During my enrollment at the school, I had two odd jobs to pay my bills. First, I drove a taxi on the weekdays. Second, I spent the weekend working as a maître d'. My classes all took place in the evenings.

Next, I moved to Fort Lauderdale and enrolled in the newly developed Doctor of Business Administration program at Nova University. I secured an appointment with the program advisor, Dr. Novak, who was very inspirational. He convinced me to apply to the program and, in September 1978, just one month after finishing my MBA, I began the doctorate program at Nova University. As usual, I began taking a full load of courses and working two jobs to afford my education and expenses.

The Iranian Revolution took place during my first year at Nova University. The old regime of the Shah of Iran was toppled after a long, bloody struggle by the Iranian people. A new revolutionary government led by Ayatollah Khomeini came to power. Many Iranians, including myself, felt the new government could benefit from the education and expertise of the younger generation. So, in February 1979, my friends and I moved back to Iran to see if we could be instrumental in helping to rebuild our country.

In the six months that I stayed there, I made numerous attempts to become involved in the development of the country—even offering to work for free. However, the country was in chaos in every aspect of life. Thus, I decided to return to the United States to complete my doctoral program.

By September 1979, I had returned to the United States to resume my doctorate. I also picked up odd jobs to support myself. This time, I managed to land a full-time job as a computer programmer at a local engineering company in Fort Lauderdale. By the spring of 1980, I had completed my course requirements at Nova University and took the comprehensive exam required to choose a major and research topic for my doctoral dissertation. After passing the exam, I decided to focus on the utilization of computer information systems (CIS) in business management.

However, I soon realized that I needed to increase my knowledge of CIS to be able to develop a comprehensive dissertation. At the time, Nova University was not offering courses in CIS, so I enrolled at my alma mater, the University of Miami. By the fall of 1980, I began taking courses at the University of Miami in the graduate CIS program. I also obtained a teaching assistance fellowship at the university, as well as teaching part time at local colleges and universities in South Florida. I completed my course load for my master's program in CIS at the University of Miami in the summer of 1981. Thus, I received my second master's degree in CIS, and, in 1982, completed my dissertation and was awarded a doctorate in business administration and information systems.

Six months prior to completing my doctoral program, I began searching for a teaching position at universities throughout the country. I received job offers from three institutions after visiting their campuses and participating in extensive interviews. The institutions included Bentley College in Boston, Ball State University in Muncie, Indiana, and the the Pennsylvania State University at Harrisburg. My doctoral advisor, Dr. Novak, convinced me to join Penn State, stating that joining such a major university would be like joining the ranks at IBM.

Based on his advice, I joined Penn State in July 1982, moving to Middletown, Pennsylvania, to be an assistant professor of information systems in the university's School of Business. My starting salary was US$28,500 a year. Ten years later, my annual salary was $33,500. I did not stay for the salary—I stayed for my love of teaching.

Six months into my tenure at Penn State, I was asked to meet with the dean of the School of Business Administration to discuss an important issue. The dean informed me that the professor who served as the current chair of the department (who also happened to be my boss) had decided to pursue her doctoral degree in computer science and, therefore, would be leaving in a few weeks. The dean had decided to appoint me as chair of the department.

I was both surprised and pleased at the offer. In fact, there were seven others, with one being employed by the university for more than 13 years and holding a degree from Harvard. The dean stated that he had witnessed my dedication and commitment to my work. In his opinion, I was the most qualified person to lead the department.

Still, I was the youngest faculty member in the School of Business. I told the dean that I was honored to be considered for the position and was proud to accept his kind offer. I went on to chair the department for 14 years, expanding the academic program with a Master of Science in Information Systems program.

In the fall of 1982, I married my girlfriend of two years, Rachel, at the Justice of the Peace in Middletown. Only a select few friends and family members were in attendance. Then, in 1988, I became a proud citizen of the United States.

I was working nearly 90 hours a week, teaching multiple courses at the undergraduate and graduate levels, conducting ongoing research in my area of expertise, managing a certificate program offered through the Continuing Education Division of Penn State, and working on computer-related programming and design projects as a consultant. At the same time, I managed to complete my first textbook, totaling more than 700 pages. The book, *Microcomputer Systems Management and Applications*, was a two-year project published by Boyd & Fraser in Boston. Its final version went through 18 rounds of expert blind reviews.

As the revision deadline neared, I had just a few days to make all my changes. I ended up revising the final version for 72 hours—without a minute of napping or rest! I worked diligently in my office from Friday morning through Saturday and into Sunday. Finally, I completed the project by Monday morning. The project proved to me that there are certain hidden abilities in all of us. We just need to challenge ourselves and those abilities will come out!

I had purchased my first condo in Coral Springs, Florida, prior to my move to Pennsylvania. I decided to rent the property, using the rental income to pay the mortgage on the condo. A year after I settled in Pennsylvania, I purchased my first house. I put down 20% of the purchase price and took out a 15-year mortgage from a local bank. As always, I paid more than the minimum monthly mortgage payment to build equity in the property. As a result of these extra payments, I had almost 40% equity in the house instead of 20% within just three years!

Next, I applied for a home equity line of credit from another local bank, using the money to put down 20% of the price of another property near our house. I took out another 15-year mortgage and used it as an investment property. The condo was immediately rented, with an income much higher than the mortgage. Thus, I paid the entire rental income to the bank as part of my plan to increase my share of the equity in the property.

After paying the mortgage on this property in an accelerated fashion, I managed to obtain a line of credit from the bank on the investment property. I used the money to purchase a parcel of land near the investment property, with plans to have a house built on it for another rental.

Regrettably, my marriage to Rachel came to an end after eight years. We went through an amicable divorce and managed to split our assets in half as part of the divorce settlement. I did, however, have to borrow money to pay her for half of the properties rather than sell them and lose money.

During the fall of 1988, in addition to teaching, I tried to find a suitable publishing house for my new academic peer-reviewed publication, *the*

Information Resources Management Journal. Upon the recommendation of my good friend and associate provost of Penn State, I formed a not-for-profit professional group, the Information Resources Management Association (IRMA), and a publishing house named Idea Group, Inc. (currently referred to as "IGI Global Scientific Publishing"). Then, Idea Group, Inc. (currently referred to as "IGI Global Scientific Publishing") could publish *the Information Resources Management Journal.*

Managing these two new entities only added to my already heavy workload, which included chairing the department at Penn State's School of Business, teaching both undergraduate and graduate courses, administrating the Penn State Continuing Education Certificate in CIS, consulting, and conducting research as part of my tenure-track professorship position. Still, the hard work paid off when Penn State granted me a tenured position as a professor, meaning my job at the university would be for life if I chose to stay.

For the next two years, I worked as hard as I could through teaching, consulting, and running Idea Group, Inc. (currently referred to as "IGI Global Scientific Publishing"). By summer 1991, I met my second wife, Beth, who was one of my former students in the Penn State Continuing Education Certificate program in CIS. After dating for two years, we got married in the spring of 1993.

Within a few years, IRMA had more than 1,000 paying members worldwide. We offered an annual international conference at different locations around the country and overseas. The event was attended by researchers in the field of information technology management who aimed to exchange ideas and innovations. IRMA published four journals through Idea Group, Inc. (currently referred to as "IGI Global Scientific Publishing"), as well as the conference proceedings from the IRMA international conference.

After several years of building Idea Group, Inc. (currently referred to as "IGI Global Scientific Publishing"), the company began publishing scholarly books. I managed to run IRMA and Idea Group, Inc. (currently referred to as "IGI Global Scientific Publishing") until the summer of 2000, when I decided to leave my academic position and become a full-time entrepreneur.

In June 2000, I left my tenured position at Penn State to run Idea Group, Inc. (currently referred to as "IGI Global Scientific Publishing") in a full-time capacity. At the time, revenue at Idea Group, Inc. (currently referred to as "IGI Global Scientific Publishing") was not enough to support me financially. Thus, for the first year, I worked at Idea Group, Inc. (currently referred to as "IGI Global Scientific Publishing") almost 90 hours a week for free.

As always, my hard work, determination to succeed, commitment, and positive attitude paid off. By the beginning of the second year, Idea Group, Inc. (currently referred to as "IGI Global Scientific Publishing") began making revenue and paying me an annual salary.

I also had the opportunity to invest in commercial real estate through Idea Group, Inc. The company was paying rent for its office space. So, in 1995, I bought an old house in Hershey and converted it into a two-story commercial building for the company. By the late 1990s, it was obvious that Idea Group, Inc. (currently referred to as "IGI Global Scientific Publishing") needed a much bigger space. I invested in two acres of land on Hershey's main street, building a two-story, 20,000-square-foot building for the publishing house. The company moved its operations to the new building in June 2001.

I'd purchased the land, paid for the construction, and put the mortgage under my name. Then, Idea Group, Inc. (currently referred to as "IGI Global Scientific Publishing") began paying me rent for the use of the office space.

The total space of the new building was more than what the company required to run its operations. Next, I found two local businesses to lease the remaining space (approximately 60% of the building) for their operations.

Three years later, Idea Group, Inc. (currently referred to as "IGI Global Scientific Publishing") expanded, needing additional space. As a result, I did not renew the lease of the other two businesses in the building. The entire building, therefore, was utilized as the headquarters of Idea Group, Inc. (currently referred to as "IGI Global Scientific Publishing").

By 2006, six years after I started Idea Group, Inc.—now named IGI Global Scientific Publishing—the company was growing significantly. We began offering digital downloads and publishing 300 books and 80 journals a year. Our audience came from all corners of the world, spanning diverse cultures, perspectives, and professional fields. In fact, almost 50% of its authors and editors came from outside of North America. At the same time, more than 50% of the company revenue was generated from overseas sales.

To better serve our international clientele, IGI Global Scientific Publishing opened an office in New York City in 2003. I purchased a 4,000-square-foot commercial condo on 35th Street between 6th Avenue and Broadway. We renovated the space into a beautiful office for IGI Global Scientific Publishing. Eventually, this office was leased to the IGI Global Scientific Publishing New York office for its operations. That same year, I also purchased a three-bedroom condo on the 50th floor of a building on 38th Street and 5th Avenue.

While things were going exceptionally well professionally, my second marriage was coming to an end. For several years, I worked out of the Hershey office before commuting by train to New York on Thursday mornings. Beth would join me on Friday afternoons, and we'd both return to Hershey on Sundays. Our plan was to move to the city full-time, making New York our home in five years. Sadly, Beth was anxious about our move, particularly due to her strong links to central Pennsylvania and her close relationship with her parents.

Our marriage ended amicably in 2010. This time, our prenuptial agreement ensured that neither of us had to give the other any portion of our assets under our own names.

While I had decided to become a full-time entrepreneur by running IGI Global Scientific Publishing, I also maintained my intellectual side by staying involved with the publisher's scholarly publications. I was the editor-in-chief of three scholarly journals and edited several books each year. I also launched a new project, the *Encyclopedia of Information Science and Technology*, in 2001. By 2003, I had completed the five-volume publication, with more than 1,000 chapters contributed by researchers from more than 50 countries.

IGI Global Scientific Publishing sold more than 1,500 copies of the publication, priced at US$1,125 per copy. Subsequently, I edited five additional editions of the publication. At the time of writing this book, I am finishing its sixth edition. After the popularity of its first edition, the number of volumes increased to 10 volumes per set and the price increased to US$6,600 per set.

Being closely involved in the work of my company not only keeps me intellectually connected to trends in the industry but also provides a sense of freedom akin to riding a bike. Just as riding allows you to navigate different paths and explore new horizons, being immersed in the day-to-day operations of the business allows me to drive forward with purpose and vision.

It helped me understand the trends and topics within the field of information science and technology. Thus, our authors and editors saw me as both a businessman and a scholar. As I've always said to my friends and colleagues, the beauty of my job is that I consider myself a musician, a composer, and the owner of the orchestra!

Losing my father in 2008 was a profound experience. I held immense respect for him; he was a resilient survivor, no matter the challenges he faced. His passing marked a significant loss in my life, but his memories became my source of strength.

Despite his physical absence, my father's presence is enduring. He visited with me in the United States often spending two weeks every six months. Each time, we would embark on a week-long journey together. These precious moments of bonding remain vivid in my mind.

Though I cannot see him, I feel his guidance and influence in my daily life. His legacy continues to shape my decisions and actions, instilling in me the values of perseverance and resilience that he embodied so well.

In the summer of 2012, I met my current wife, Olga, in the waiting area of my attorney's office. While I was seated, a young woman walked in and asked the receptionist to see another attorney from the firm. She was asked to wait until that attorney became available. As we waited to see our respective lawyers, we began talking. Olga told me she was from Russia and had an accounting degree from the City University of New York. She was currently working for an accounting firm. I mentioned to her that I was a former professor at Penn State University (knowing that her culture held professors in high regard). Before we departed, I wrote my cell phone number on the back of my business card and handed it to her.

Honestly, I was not expecting to hear from her due to our age difference. Surprisingly, Olga contacted me two days later—and the rest is history. We dated for almost a year and a half before I proposed. She accepted and, in November 2015, we got married at the top of the Freedom Tower in Manhattan.

A year later, Olga gave me a son, Darius, named after Darius the Great of the Persian Empire. Three years later, we welcomed another handsome son, Cyrus, named after another famous king of the Persian Empire, Cyrus the Great. By August 2019, we purchased a five-bedroom condo on the 60th floor of a new high-rise building only a block from the Freedom Tower in downtown Manhattan.

IGI Global Scientific Publishing continues to expand. By April 2018, we opened a subsidiary, IGI Science and Technology, Ltd., in Beijing, with a managing director and three staff members who work to expand our steadily growing market share in China. By the end of 2018, IGI Global Scientific Publishing was publishing more than 500 books a year, 175 scholarly journals, and a dozen databases.

The IGI Global Scientific Publishing brand was also becoming accepted by the research and academic library communities and recognized as a high-quality, reliable, independent international academic publishing house. We published scientific and scholarly books on three major academic topics: (a) business and management; (b) technical, scientific, and medical; and (c) education. By 2004, the company was publishing 800 books annually, 200 journals, and two dozen databases.

By 2025, the company aims to publish 1,000 books and 250 journals. Then, in 2026, IGI Global Scientific Publishing will publish 1,250 books and nearly 300 journals.

Today, IGI Global Scientific Publishing is recognized and respected by researchers across the world, as well as academic librarians. Our books are regularly purchased by academic librarians from premier research institutions like Harvard University, Princeton, the University of Sydney in Australia, the University of Pennsylvania, Cambridge University, and Massachusetts Institute of Technology.

I strongly advocate for acquiring knowledge and embracing lifelong learning as essential components of personal and professional development. The pursuit of knowledge allows us to continuously expand our understanding, skills, and perspective. In addition, education should not be confined to formal settings. Whether through formal or informal education, each opportunity enhances our capabilities.

Challenges are crucial for growth. Thus, we should push ourselves beyond our comfort zones to unlock our full potential. By confronting challenges, we can discover hidden talents, develop resilience, and achieve our goals.

As mentioned in this book, the main difference between human animals and other animals is the fact that humans are capable of utilizing their intelligence to reason and make logical sense of things around them. A human newborn's intelligence and knowledge base—the brain—is empty except for intuitive directions. Throughout our upbringing, we try to expand our knowledge base, and ultimately, our intelligence benefits from both formal and informal knowledge.

The primary source of obtaining formal knowledge is the educational path and becoming a life-long professional learner. Accessible formal knowledge includes judgment, intuition, hunches, experience, feelings, emotions, smell, sound, taste, and visual. Some of these are parts of humans' main senses. Others, such as judgment, are perfected based on experiences gained in life. Sometimes, the informal information that we use is referred to as common sense or street smarts. Obtaining an abundance of both formal and informal knowledge is the fuel to our success in every aspect of life.

In terms of human differences, we are all born with certain strengths and weaknesses. Our goal in life should be to enhance our strengths and improve our weaknesses. One should not assume that we cannot achieve these two goals. Instead, we need to strive to become better and stronger.

Earlier, I talked about human needs by referencing Maslow's hierarchy of needs. Physiological needs, which are found at the bottom of his pyramid, include food, water, and air. The next level, the issue of safety, includes a safe place to work and a safe place to live. Then, the hierarchy moves on to the level of love and belonging. These are important human connections, helping us feel wanted and valued, whether through family, neighbors, or other close groups. Esteem is the next level, with reference to self-esteem, self-worth, and one's ability to achieve positive objectives. The final level of the pyramid is self-actualization. This can be thought of as the realization of one's creative, intellectual, and social potential through accomplishments like earning money, status, or power.

In general, one must look for opportunities and address obstacles within all levels of Maslow's hierarchy. As I mentioned on numerous occasions in this book, opportunities are not given. Instead, they are earned. It is up to the individual to utilize their knowledge and intellectual ability to analyze situations or circumstances to identify beneficial opportunities.

In terms of obstacles, life is full of challenges. Thus, one should always be prepared to face obstacles with a positive attitude and determination. For instance, we have two options when describing a glass with only half of its water. A person with a positive attitude will describe it as half full. A person with a negative attitude will describe it as half empty.

In terms of human capabilities, most studies have indicated that people only utilize 20% to 25% of their physical and mental capabilities. However, it is just a matter of time or a specific situation that helps you access additional capabilities.

For instance, I often ask people what level of swimming they possess. If someone says "average" or "enough to float," I ask them what happens if they fall out of a boat in the middle of the deepest ocean. Their response: I don't know! My answer, however, would be that you will begin to swim in a way that you never knew you could swim. You will be fighting for your life—you will be trying to survive. As a result, a certain energy kicks in and calls forward your hidden ability.

Athletes, through training and challenging themselves, end up accessing those hidden abilities. Therefore, you should not question your capability to achieve certain goals. Instead, you should challenge yourself to bring those hidden abilities forward—like the night I worked 72 hours without sleep to finish my final 700-page manuscript or the time I ran a half marathon. Prior to that race, the longest I'd ever run was just six miles. Still, on the morning of the marathon, I was determined to achieve my goal of running 13.1 miles in the shortest amount of time. Eventually, I finished in one hour and 56 minutes, which was in the 30 percentile. And I received a medal!

One contributing factor for a successful, happy life is effective time management. It maximizes productivity, reduces stress, and allows individuals to prioritize activities that bring them joy and satisfaction. Regrettably, many people underestimate the value of time and time management. Instead, we should look at time in the same fashion in which we view money.

Imagine if every week we are given $156,000 (7 days x 24 hours x $1,000 = value of each hour). Would we just spend this money carelessly without any concerns about how we can benefit from it?

Many people find that working any more than the regular 40-hour workweek (that we are brainwashed to follow) would be a crime. In reality, working harder is one way to compete with others in settings like college courses or at work. Yes, that means working a bit more than your usual 40 hours a week.

If you designate these 40 hours as $40,000 from the weekly $156,000 that you're given each week, it is not even one-third of the total amount. At the same time, studies indicate that younger generations spend up to six hours or $60,000 a day on social media, without seeing a return on the time or money invested in it. At least the 40 hours or $40,000 a week at work bring a monetary reward and support your way of living!

So, if you manage your time carefully, you can achieve a great deal and get ahead of others. You can live comfortably and have fun. And that is exactly how I live my life. Even on those days that I was working 90 hours a week (or spending $90,000 a week), I was not living a miserable life. In fact, I knew I was working on building the foundation of my future!

As they say—no pain, no gain!

Beyond the publishing world, I strongly believe in the importance of giving back. Using our connections and abilities to help those in need is not just a responsibility but a core value that drives meaningful impact and positive change in our world.

Success isn't just measured by professional achievements but also by the positive influence we can have on the lives of others. Whether through charitable initiatives, mentorship, or partnerships with other organizations, we should strive to make a difference beyond our immediate sphere of influence.

The act of giving to others should be viewed as a part of our human obligation. As mentioned in the poem "Bani Adam" (The Children of Adam) by the famous Persian poet Saadi Shirazi from the 13th century, "The children of Adam are limbs of each other, having been created of one essence. When the calamity of time affects one limb, the other limbs cannot remain at rest. If you have no sympathy for the troubles and pains of others, you are unworthy to be called by the name of a Human."

As a child, my father taught me the act of helping others. Although my father did not have much to share because he had to feed his large family, he would still find many ways to help.

I began assisting in any way I could once I became more financially secure. For instance, I contributed to a variety of charitable organizations, as well as volunteering to work in hospital settings or soup kitchens.

I used to dream of the day that I could build a hospital in poor neighborhoods in northern Iran. I wanted to offer care for poor children. This dream never left my system!

In 2003, I decided to make my dream a reality. Together with my legal and financial teams, I created a non-profit, the World Forgotten Children Foundation (WFCF), to help orphaned children with disabilities in poor countries across the world. Over the past 20 years, WFCF has been able to fund global projects in countries like Haiti, Ukraine, Zambia, and China, assisting children with disabilities and improving the quality of their lives.

Almost 99.9% of the financial support of WFCF comes from my family and my company, IGI Global Scientific Publishing. It makes me so happy that I can fulfill my longstanding dream of helping poor children with disabilities throughout the world!

In life, we decide how to prepare ourselves to succeed. It is the responsibility of no one else! We direct our destiny. As a teenager, I decided that I would not accept the life of a shop keeper like so many other young men were resigning themselves to do. Instead, I purposefully chose to pursue my education in a non-traditional way. I knew that I would face challenges related to finances, time, and my level of maturity. I also knew that without a good education, my chances of success would be very slim. The only way for me to break out of that situation was to get my education. If there is a will, there is a way!

Eventually, through all the obstacles and barriers that I dealt with in my personal life, I defined my ultimate equation for success:

Success = Intelligence + Hard Work + Determination + Commitment + Positive Attitude

I believe that hard work is the most crucial element within this equation. And, if you read autobiographies of successful people like Bill Gates, Steve Jobs, Warren Buffet, and Jeff Bezos, they have one thing in common: They all worked hard, long hours to get where they are in their lives.

Finally, through success comes freedom. This is defined as the power or privilege to speak and act freely without any constraints or restrictions. Freedom is often associated with liberty and autonomy in how one chooses to live one's life without being controlled. Obviously, in a free society, there are different types of freedom, including freedom to read, freedom to move, freedom to listen, freedom to travel, and freedom to love.

Most free societies also offer financial freedom. This privilege controls almost all other types of freedom: what to eat, what to read, what to watch, and where to live. Therefore, it is extremely important to plan and manage your financial resources as effectively as possible to achieve financial security.

To create ultimate financial security, you must make plans at an early stage of your adult life. You must be mindful that secure and thriving financial freedom does not occur overnight unless you have inherited the financial resources. Regardless, you must be cognizant of effective financial management because the assets can disappear very quickly.

Investing in future financial freedom requires certain sacrifices, like foregoing a trendy $5 coffee when you are living paycheck to paycheck. Instead, you should purchase a cup of coffee from McDonald's.

Accumulating wealth is not that difficult if you plan and practice from a young age. For instance, I planned my financial freedom as a young man. Even when I was attending college, I kept my personal expenses down and increased my earnings to pay for tuition.

Later in life, I learned that the strongest and safest investment is through real estate. This knowledge allowed me to build equity on my properties, as well as borrow money from the bank based on the equities within each property. Then, I could use the borrowed money to invest in another property and pay the collected rent toward the mortgage. This formula was very effective, permitting me to create a robust real estate portfolio worth millions of dollars.

In conclusion, our lives are shaped by the decisions we make and the actions we take. It is through hard work and perseverance that we forge our own paths forward, realizing freedom and opportunities. Embracing innovation and thinking outside the box are essential in navigating challenges and seizing opportunities along the way.

By staying committed to our goals, maintaining resilience in the face of obstacles, and seeking new ways to grow, we empower ourselves to create meaningful, freer lives. Each decision to push boundaries, innovate, and persist brings us closer to realizing our aspirations and making a positive impact on ourselves and the world around us.

My ultimate hope in writing this book about my life story and philosophy is to teach my two sons, Darius and Cyrus, the same values my father taught me. Obviously, the circumstances surrounding their lives are 100% different than my own. However, there are core beliefs that I want to pass on to them.

First, hard work is the cornerstone of success, driving us to achieve our goals. Second, appreciate what you have and how you can live your life. It is a privilege that should keep you motivated. Third, step out of your comfort zone, challenging yourself to discover your hidden abilities and strengths. Fourth, education opens doors and will empower you to make meaningful contributions. Understand the value of knowledge and commit to becoming a lifelong learner. Lastly, understand that it is your responsibility to give back and help those less fortunate people in this world. Acts of kindness foster a compassionate society and will enrich your own lives.

I am also grateful for my father's lessons and the opportunities to watch him demonstrate a life of hard work, resilience, and outreach. While my own life's journey has included many obstacles and avenues, Dad has been my driving force. His confidence in the face of adversity taught me to be unrelenting in my pursuits Through his work ethic, I learned to push myself beyond my limits. And his examples continue to be a source of motivation that I am proud to pass down to his grandsons. His legacy will be a guiding light for future generations.

By reading about my experiences, you, too, can learn ways to overcome challenges in this life and seize new opportunities. As a boy, I dreamed of owning a used bicycle, a dream that was quickly dashed after I misspoke. Yet, my journey is solid proof that each of us can shape our own paths and achieve our goals through resilience and hard work. By choosing determination and knowledge, you can achieve your dreams.

Indexing

Abraham Maslow, 180
Accumulating wealth, 202, 205, 254
Affluent, 211
African Community Project, 222
American University, 10, 59, 150, 152
American University in Cairo, 152
Baby Box Church, 223–224
Bachelor's degree, 89, 92, 97, 101, 104, 130, 134–135, 149, 179, 237–238
Beijing, 159, 172, 247
Believe Project, 221–222
Bethesda Mission, 215
Bicycle, 1–2, 9–10, 14, 21, 51, 173, 211, 216, 255
Books, 28, 41, 107, 109, 128, 152, 157-158, 161–162, 164, 167, 170, 199, 233, 243–245, 247–248
Boyd & Fraser Publishing Company, 146
Broward Community College, 128–129, 131, 145, 205
Business administration, 87, 101, 104–105, 112, 117, 132, 135, 160, 211, 237–241
Center of Mobility and Stimulation of Children with Disabilities, 222
Chair, 10, 30, 125, 131, 135, 137–138, 141, 143, 241
China, 81, 88, 159, 171–172, 217, 224–225, 247, 252
Citizen, 147–148, 196, 241
Conference proceedings, 152, 158, 243
Continuing Education, 140, 241, 243
COVID-19, 225–226
Curriculum, 140, 145
Cyrus the Great, 174–175, 247
Darius the Great, 173–174, 247
Debt, 44, 150, 185, 202, 233
Department of CIS, 137, 150
Developing countries, 216, 228
Diema's Dream Foundation, 221
Digital revolution, 192
Disabilities, 217–218, 222, 225, 228, 252
Discipline, 65, 137, 192
Doctoral degree, 112, 116, 118, 130, 132, 134, 137, 160, 241
Doctoral program, 113, 116, 122, 125, 131, 134, 239–240

Doctoral studies, 113
Dokimoi Ergatai program, 219
Economic conditions, 217
Economy, 114, 117, 186
EContent Pro, 1–2, 170
EContent Pro International, 1–2
Encyclopedia, 152, 245
Equity, 148–149, 151, 158, 206–208, 242, 254
Faculty, 112, 134–135, 137–145, 148, 150, 159, 241
Financial freedom, 11, 175, 197–200, 211, 253–254
FORTRAN, 125–126, 137
GED, 51, 53, 58–59, 127, 130, 148, 179, 215, 235–236
Gilan Province, 24, 32
GP6D, 233
Graduate school, 106, 112, 124, 131
Handbooks of research, 152
Harrisburg, 134–135, 146–148, 150–151, 158, 206, 208, 215, 240
Harrisburg Area Community College, 148
Hershey, 1–2, 148, 150–151, 157–158, 160, 162, 165, 208–209, 215, 244–245
Hershey Lodge and Convention Center, 157
Hierarchy of human needs, 180, 191
Hyojin Kim Nirav Patel Foundation, 224
Idea Group, Inc., 156–165, 208–210, 243-244
IGI Global Scientific Publishing, 165–172, 209, 244–248, 252
IGI Science, Ltd., 172
Immigration, 77
Income, 16, 27, 29, 48, 141, 149–150, 159, 200, 202–206, 208, 210, 217, 236, 242
Information Resources Management Association (IRMA), 156, 243
Information Resources Management Journal (IRMJ), 154, 243
International Catholic Child Bureau, 222
International China Concern (ICC), 225
Investment, 149, 151, 161, 192, 198, 204, 208–210, 242, 254
Iranian Revolution, 69, 113, 115, 239
IRMA, 156–157, 161, 164, 243
IRMJ, 154, 156, 167, 243
Islamic Republic, 114
Journal of Database Management, 157
Journal of End User Computing, 157
Journal of Global Information Management, 157
Journals, 141, 152, 157–158, 161–162, 164, 167, 170, 243–245, 247–248

Kocebuka Community Foundation, 225
Kuwait University, 152
Library, 2, 49, 103, 107, 123, 129, 212, 247
Loyola University, 149
Machine languages, 142
Management, 101–102, 106, 108, 112, 117, 123, 128, 131, 137, 145–146, 154, 156–157, 161, 164, 168–170, 188, 190, 194, 200–202, 227, 238, 240–241, 243, 248, 250, 253
Master's degree, 118, 124–125, 130, 149, 240
MBA program, 105–107, 116, 143, 151, 238
MBA programs 105, 112
McDonald's, 82, 84, 88, 106, 125, 176, 205, 237
Mercedes Benz, 55, 211
Mercy & Sharing, 220
Messiah University, 219
Miami Dade, 71, 77, 81, 85, 87, 99, 104, 124, 126, 237–238
Miami Dade Community College, 77, 85, 87, 104, 124, 237
Microcomputer Systems Management and Applications, 146, 241
Military, 63, 79, 106, 114–115, 119, 137, 237
Military government, 114
MKP Technologies, 169–170
Mobility equipment, 225
Mortgage 148-149, 151, 158, 162, 165, 205–210, 242, 244, 254
National Autonomous University of Mexico, 152
New York City, 5, 54, 165–166, 173, 175, 209, 211, 214, 245
Non-profit, 156, 215, 218–220, 228, 252
Nova Southeastern University, 112, 128, 131–132
Nova University, 112, 117, 239–240
Orphanages, 217, 220, 223–225
Pahlavi dynasty, 113, 116
Peer-reviewed, 152, 154, 156–157, 170, 243
Penn State, 134–138, 141–142, 144, 146, 148–149, 154, 157, 167, 172, 192, 206, 211, 215, 240–241, 243–244, 247
Pennsylvania, 5, 98, 112, 134–136, 138, 147, 149–151, 154, 156, 165–167, 175, 205–206, 209, 215, 240, 242, 245, 248
Pennsylvania State University, 134, 240
PhD, 138
Porsche, 211
Professors, 107, 112, 128, 135, 141, 144, 152, 247
Programmer, 125–127, 129, 239
Properties, 175, 202, 209–211, 242, 254

Protests, 113
Publishing, 146, 154–155, 157–159, 161, 163–172, 209, 211, 243–248, 251–252
Racism, 88-89, 237
Real estate, 119, 149, 159, 162–153, 172, 175, 202, 204, 208–210, 244, 254
Rental, 150, 175, 208, 210–211, 242
Researchers, 152, 154, 157–158, 170, 243, 245, 248
Research institutions, 112, 248
Resistance, 145
Retirement, 150, 212
Revolutionary government, 114, 239
Sabbatical, 137, 150
Salary, 51, 134–135, 162, 205–206, 240, 244
Shah, 31-32, 61, 69, 113-116, 118, 121, 239
Stereotyping, 136
Students, 51, 60, 71, 79, 82, 85–86, 98, 101–103, 105–108, 112, 127–128, 134–135, 140–145, 149, 151–152, 155, 167, 186, 189, 235, 238, 243
Sustainable practices, 218, 227
Tehran, 14–16, 25–26, 28, 30, 32, 38, 42–44, 54–55, 60, 63, 68–72, 77, 83–84, 102, 113, 117–118, 120–122, 136, 152, 166, 179, 190, 215–216, 232–234, 236
Tenure, 134, 137, 141–144, 163, 241
Theocracy, 113
Tuition, 51, 59, 100, 106, 124, 129, 148, 190, 199, 201, 237–238, 254
UNICEF, 216–217, 227
UNESCO, 219
United States, 2, 94, 115, 212, 241
University of Carlos III of de Madrid, 152
University of Miami, 99–100, 102, 104–105, 124, 126, 128, 135, 238, 240
University of Tehran, 60, 113, 152
University of the West Indies, 152
University of Wollongong, 152
Washington, D.C., 72, 150–151
Work ethic, 104, 137, 255
World Forgotten Children Foundation (WFCF), 218, 228, 252

www.ingramcontent.com/pod-product-compliance
Lightning Source LLC
Chambersburg PA
CBHW080746060526
44119CB00072B/167